I BEG TO DIFFER

I BEG TO DIFFER

POLITICALLY INCORRECT, PROUDLY MIDWESTERN, POTENTIALLY FUNNY

by Laura Pulfer

ORANGE FRAZER *PRESS*
Wilmington, Ohio, USA
1998

ISBN 1-882203-24-0
Copyright 1998 by Laura Pulfer

Additional copies of I Beg to Differ, Politically Incorrect, Proudly Midwestern, Potentially Funny or other Orange Frazer Press publications may be ordered directly from:

Orange Frazer Press, Inc.
Box 214
37 ¹/₂ West Main Street
Wilmington, Ohio 45177

Telephone 1.800.852.9332 for price and shipping information
Web Site: www.orangefrazer.com;
E-mail address: editor@orangefrazer.com

Library of Congress Cataloging-in-Publication Data
Pulfer, Laura. 1946-
    I beg to differ : politically incorrect, proudly Midwestern, potentially funny / by Laura Pulfer.
        p.   cm.
    Collection of newspaper columns originally published in the Cincinnati enquirer. 1995-1997.
    ISBN 1-882203-24-0
    1. Pulfer, Laura, 1946-   . 2. Women journalists--United States--Biography. 3. Radio broadcasters--United States--Biography. I. Title.
PN4874.P79A3   1998
070'.92--dc21
    [b]   98-26623
                                                           CIP

*To the memory
of my first editor and mentor,
Hope Strong, who taught me
what I needed to know to make
my living as a writer.*

*And to my mother,
Betty Rose Archer,
who taught me
everything else.*

TABLE OF CONTENTS

MOTHERS AND OTHER HEROES

SEXUAL POLITICS MAKE
STRANGE BEDFELLOWS

SEASON'S GREETINGS:
HO-HO-HO, HABARAGANI AND BOO

YOUR TAX DOLLARS
AND OTHER TOXIC WASTE

THE DAYS OF WHINE AND NOSES

TRAVELS TO UNFAMILIAR PLACES,
SUCH AS OUTER SPACE

CONTEMPLATING MIDDLE-AGED NAVELS

I BEG TO DIFFER

IF THE MEDIUM IS THE MESSAGE, WHAT ARE THEY TRYING TO SAY?

CHAPTERS FROM THE NOSEBLEED FILES

WINNING THE HUMAN RACE

SMALL, UNFORGIVABLE LOSSES

ACKNOWLEDGEMENTS

THANKS TO JAN Leach, Larry Beaupre and Harry Whipple of *The Cincinnati Enquirer*, who supported me when they liked what I had to say. And also when they didn't. Everything, except for the radio commentaries, is reprinted from *The Enquirer* with their permission. There have been some modest changes to reflect the passage of time and events.

I'm grateful to Mary Jo DiLonardo, Julie Irwin, Anne Michaud, Brian Gregg, Lisa Donovan, Ben Kaufman, Kristen DelGuzzi, Lucy May, Laura Goldberg and Howard Wilkinson for friendship, tips and advice. Wonderful reporters all, they are responsible for the things that are true and good that I wouldn't have known otherwise.

Lorna Jordan is to blame for my radio career. Thank you, Lorna, for making me say it until you could "hear the smile." And thanks to Greg Allen, senior editor of National Public Radio's *Morning Edition*, who let me smile nationwide.

I must also recognize Frank Shue, who says some remarkably funny things I am too proud to steal, except in an emergency. My dear friend, Jan Annett, is my guru in children's matters, my daughter Meg in matters of the heart.

Mike Pulfer is my best husband, co-parent, lover, confidant, advisor and, not incidentally, editor.

The really stupid stuff I did all by myself.

PREFACE

WHEN I'M FEELING full of myself, I tell people I'm a writer. The truth is that I'm just a person with a notebook and a lot of questions. And when I get the answers, I can't wait to spill it to somebody else.

Some readers have told me they think I'm funny. I think the world can be a funny place and, sometimes, on a good day, I can describe it well enough to make you laugh.

I hope this is a good day.

Laura Pulfer
Cincinnati, 1998

I BEG TO DIFFER

One

LIFE NOTICES AND
NO-GUN SALUTES

*"I want my children to
have an understanding of
people's hopes and dreams."*
—Diana, Princess of Wales

THE MEN WHO BECAME OUR FATHERS

IT WAS EXACTLY as terrible as I thought it might be.

My father was seventy-one, and, as a decorated World War II veteran, was eligible for a full military ceremony at the cemetery. Mom said okay to everything but the guns.

It had been a half century since my father's military adventures in Europe, where he joined a tour of Hitler's death camps, ordered by Gen. Dwight D. Eisenhower, "so the world will never forget." Now, he rests on a little hill overlooking the oil refinery in Lima, Ohio, where he worked for thirty-six years. The icon of the plant is an immense torch, which burns off waste. Dad's eternal flame, my brother said.

My father's most recent military service was conducted by the men of VFW Post two hundred five. Their hands shook, and they fumbled a little bit — quite a bit — as they folded the flag. They managed a semi-crisp salute to my mother as they handed it over to her, but it was still hard to imagine them as the heroes of Normandy and Iwo Jima.

It's easier to imagine them as the heroes of Lima and Cincinnati and Detroit and Milwaukee. Which they were.

During those fifty years after they got home from the war, my father's generation was rearing mine. And doing a rather heroic job, if I do say so.

No matter how you cut it, my fellow sisters, these guys are the generation who made it safe for us to shoot our mouths off. However baffled they were by the way the world was changing, they came home from the war and went back to work and helped our mothers liberate us, which my father said was considerably more complicated than liberating Paris.

They sent us off to college and endured our homecoming when, like other generations before us, we knew everything there was to know about everything. But, unlike their generation, we were not too polite to say so. They endured our hair and significant-other sleepovers.

Generation-X and the generation in training will be happy to tell you how tough it is to grow up these days. Drugs. AIDS. The occasional television without a remote. It you ask those of us who grew up during the nineteen fifties, most of us will tell you it was terrific. We were impossibly innocent. And safe. And important.

It was before Francis Gary Powers, when we found out that we spy. And before John F. Kennedy and Vietnam and Richard Nixon and Phil Donahue, when we found out worse things. We may have been living in a fool's paradise, but it still felt like paradise to us fools.

My father refused job promotions in other cities because he and my mother did not want their children to have to change schools. They never missed a piano recital or a sporting event that featured any of their children. Even if that child's participation was from the bench. Oddly, my father's career prospered.

As we buried him, I looked around at the men of his generation who survive him. They're not like us.

They lived by the rules. We pride ourselves on being flexible. Boy, are we flexible. Flexible mortgage rates. Flexible securities. Flexible living arrangements. Flexible hours. Flexible morals.

Just so you won't think this is entirely about my own, personal father and maybe convince you it's a little bit about yours, I'll borrow from May Sarton in *At Seventy: A Journal:* "We are never done thinking about our parents, I suppose, and come to know them better long after they are dead than we ever did when they were alive."

— *October, 1995*

THE CASE FOR SPEAKING UP WHILE YOU CAN

MONICA NOLAN DIED before I learned enough to tell her these things:

1. I'm sorry I used to squirm when you created scenes at important male institutions.

I was young. She was not. She was smart. I was not. I thought if I was gracious and logical, I could persuade powerful men to do the right thing. She understood power. "It's like a muscle, Dear," she told me once. "If you want it to grow, you have to exercise it."

She was the first woman to do many things in Cincinnati. Like a generation of today's career women, I came in on her coattails. The men who finally allowed us entry probably liked me better. I never caused them a moment's trouble, and I never raised my voice.

She did. Every chance she got.

Once, somebody at a private club suggested cheaper membership fees for women. And didn't Monica — who'd been the first female member — throw a fit. The men around the table at that august institution were astonished. (I was busy squirming.) They thought they were being generous, even enlightened.

Monica enlightened them. She told them what they ought to do is pay their female employees a living wage. She said there were plenty of women supporting families, and their biggest problem was not coming up with the price of a business-club membership. She said a lower membership fee was admission — and she said this with a great, big aha! in her voice — that they weren't paying women what they were worth.

She actually shook her finger at the president of a bank, something I would never do.

2. I'm sorry you were never my stockbroker.

I'm guessing she was as good at picking winners as she was at everything else. Maybe I'd be sunning myself on my yacht by now if I'd had sense enough to ask for her help. At worst, I could have put my money where her mouth was. You can bet that she used female professionals every chance she got.

3. I'm sorry I was too chicken to play tennis with you.

She played basketball, field hockey and baseball at the University of Cincinnati, where she graduated in nineteen forty-two. And tennis. World War II cheated her out of a berth at Wimbledon, but she played a ferocious game well into her sixties. She would have squashed me like a bug.

By the way, instead of whining about her missed opportunity, she threw herself into the war effort and served for five years in Greenland, India and Europe in the Red Cross.

4. I'm sorry I didn't pester you with questions.

I noticed that her obituary called her Miss Nolan. I wonder if she would have liked that. I don't remember ever hearing anybody call her Ms. She certainly was a feminist, one of the first real ones I ever met. She most certainly was not liberated because she was never not free.

I wonder how she got to know the Kennedys. They were great friends, and Jack came to town for a fund-raiser when Monica ran unsuccessfully for Congress. And wouldn't she have whipped that bunch into shape.

5. I'm sorry I never said thanks.

— *December, 1995*

FIFI: STREET PERSON WITH STYLE

WORD MADE ITS way slowly across town, from the soup kitchens to the corner offices. Fifi was gone.

Fifi Taft Rockefeller, the undisputed queen of the street, was dead after eighty-one incandescent years. Struggling to put a name to the vivid and noisy display that was Fifi, some have described her as a bag lady. She was never that. And she was never homeless.

A character. That's what she was on a good day. Loud, opinionated, persistent, confusing, fragrant. On a bad day, she was considerably more charming in the abstract than in person. "The Feef," as she was known around the courthouse, where she was a fixture for three decades, was famous for her indecipherable political rampages and her indescribable wardrobe. Sequins, white silk gloves, a squirrel stole, hats and visors.

In nineteen eighty, a *Newsweek* reporter at the Republican National Convention was startled to see a woman in a green wig, wearing a wristwatch on her ankle. Back in Cincinnati, we knew immediately that Fifi had taken her politics on the road. She ran for president several times and governor of Kentucky once. If Fifi weren't so scrambled, she could have ruled the world.

Before the city opened shelters for the homeless in the nineteen seventies, Fifi attended court every Saturday morning to post bond for drunks locked up the night before. They'd follow her home, where they'd sign a power of attorney allowing her to cash their government checks.

"They became totally dependent on the Feef for money," says Judge Deidra Hair. "The Feef genuinely meant well, like a scruffy Peter Pan. Everything she did was for the good of her lost boys." She used to tell people that she had a baby by Ronald Reagan and another by Elvis. She loved men, and flirted with the funeral director while she was making arrangements to cremate the man she lived with for twenty-eight years. Her real baby is Gay, a lovely middle-aged dental hygienist who must be the most tolerant daughter who ever drew breath.

Gay was placed in a foster home when her mother was committed to a mental hospital. Fifi tied some bed sheets together, left through a window, stole an ambulance and retrieved her daughter. "When I was really little, we hitchhiked to Illinois. She took me to burlesque shows in Indianapolis, Cincinnati and St. Louis."

This kind and forgiving woman had her mother cremated and helped plan a service at her mother's favorite soup kitchen. People there repeated Fifi stories. About bailing the drunks out of jail. About her sensational fashion flair. About her practice of mooning construction workers. About her last day, when the hospital chaplain asked what he could do for her.

"How about a kiss, Honey?"

Exasperating? You bet.

Indomitable? To the end.

— *August, 1997*

THE PEOPLE'S PRINCESS

DID WE ADORE Diana to death? Her brother thinks we did, all of us, with our insatiable interest in her life. We can hardly be blamed, can we? Who would not be fascinated by a privileged child who chose to become a woman of substance? Who would not love a princess who left the ball to go to a hospice? Who would not admire someone who touched the hands of the dying while the rest of the world looked away?

"With one royal handshake given to a young man with AIDS in the late nineteen eighties, Diana forever changed the face of AIDS for the world," says David Harvey of the national AIDS Policy Center for Children, Youth and Family.

Who would not like to know more about this princess who coltishly stepped from the back seat of the Bentley limo to shake hands, to hug, to smile? And, just this once, can we not make her a victim? Or a saint?

She was a woman with, according to Henry Kissinger, "a wicked sense of humor." She was vain enough to sweat in a gym to shape the body she draped with hundreds of thousands of dollars worth of glamorous gowns.

At one time, she was bulimic, at another, she attempted suicide. She giggled when she was supposed to be solemn. She was headstrong. She cried in public. She had a lover while she was married. She blabbed to the press. She was, in short, a very human being.

Does anybody believe that nineteen-year-old Lady Diana Frances Spencer knew what she was walking into when she said yes to the heir apparent to the throne of England? Did she know that she was signing up to be the trophy wife of a man who had no intention of giving up his mistress?

Did she understand that her in-laws were not hoping she would find a place for herself in their world? They had the place already picked out. Ribboncutter. Decoration on the arm of the monarch-to-be. And, most important of all, she was expected to produce a little king.

Did this doe-eyed child, a kindergarten teacher's aid, understand that she was being recruited as a breeder? And what a good breeder she was, quickly producing the "heir and a spare." It was then, I think, that she became the person so mourned by the world. She became a good mother as well as a good person.

Did she continue her good works with such a vengeance because she wanted to set an example for her boys? Where did she find the courage to buck the English monarchy to rear her boys with love as well as a sense of duty?

"I want my children to have an understanding of people's emotions, of people's hopes and dreams," she told a reporter. When I heard the news of her death, I admit that I did not immediately wonder about the fate of the royal House of Windsor or the laws governing photo-thugs. I wondered who would tell Harry and Wills that they had lost the warmth in their lives.

And I wondered if anybody would let them cry.

A British commentator says Prince Charles may forever be blamed for the tragedy of her life. For certain, we will be watching the Royals. They had better fly their flags at half staff. They had better get off their horses. They had better take good care of Diana's boys. And they had better look at least as sad as the rest of us feel.

If they'd like to keep their jobs in what Prince Charles calls the "family firm," they should have been paying more attention to her. She chose people, and they chose her right back. Princess Diana, pulled into the family business sixteen years ago, made a real job for herself, refused to be window dressing and refused to be fired. In the end, she understood leadership.

We want our royalty to be better than we are. Not better clothes, not better jewels. But better people. If the British ruling family — those stiff and chilly Windsors — cannot bring themselves to honor her as a princess, perhaps they can follow the lead of us commoners. Perhaps they will honor her as a person.

— *September, 1997*

A Promise Kept

HEREWITH AN ACCOUNT of an unusually brave life. Cancer, multiple sclerosis. Sometimes it must have been tough just to summon up enough breath to smile. Yet smile she did. And most of us who knew Nancy Janes Boothe cannot summon up any other expression in her memory.

Her wheelchair became a fixture at charitable events, receptions, VIP dinners, at her church. The wheelchair, of course, didn't get there by itself. Leon Boothe, her husband of thirty-seven years, was behind her. Fitting, when you think about it, because she was behind him for so many years. She taught school while he earned his advanced degrees, then was a full-time mom when he went to work. He came to Northern Kentucky University in nineteen eighty-three as its third president.

Not yet thirty years old, this college in Highland Heights, with its beigy poured concrete buildings and low foliage, looks like the upstart it is. The president's house overlooks the college the Boothes built. Both of them. As their three daughters grew and left home, Nancy Boothe stepped from behind her husband and took her place at his side.

NKU's "first lady" sampled cafeteria food and rescued wallflowers. She chaired committees and served on boards. This was a woman, after all, who had registered black voters in Mississippi during the early nineteen sixties. Goodness, I suppose, is a hard habit to break.

Although she was diagnosed with multiple sclerosis just before they came to NKU, for many years she was unimpeded by the disease. Then she became a little wobbly. She told her husband she thought it was time to tell people about her MS. Then she more or less ignored it, determined, her husband says, "to live life to its fullest and to be with people." The Boothes traveled. They worked. Nancy helped more people from a wheelchair than most of us will ever do on two legs.

You saw them everywhere. There was an unofficial drill. Leon would push his wife's chair into a room and find a good spot to park it. Then he'd troll the room, letting us know where to find Nancy. He did that for our benefit, not for hers.

Toward the end, Nancy lost the use of her arms, but never her voice or her mind. Her husband would feed her. Sometimes at the head table, sometimes in front of a thousand people. And this lovely and dignified woman would let him.

The Boothes liked me enough to invite me to their daughter's wedding a few years ago. And I liked them enough to go. It was a beautiful ceremony. And I remember wondering if the kids in the wedding party, including the bride and groom, really understood the pact made that day.

Because there were two people in that church who did.

For richer, for poorer.

In sickness and in health.

Leon and Nancy memorized the traditional vows for their wedding, and he spoke those words again to his wife as she lay dying. The last sound she heard was her husband's voice repeating that promise kept. When I hear Mendelssohn's wedding march, the picture I will always have is not of Alençon lace and a bridal veil, young men in rented tuxedos. It is the indelible memory of a woman in a wheelchair, her head cocked to smile at the silver-haired man behind her.

— *January, 1997*

THE FINAL, BEST LESSON

SEVERAL YEARS AGO, I was invited to a dinner party, a small one, and I knew that Joseph Bernardin would be among the guests. Naturally, I worried about all the wrong things. A non-Catholic, I wondered what you were supposed to call the man who was then archbishop. He told me "Father" still sounded pretty good to him. And what, I fidgeted, would we talk about? I was still young, but somehow I summoned up enough sense to listen instead of talk when I was seated next to him at dinner.

A lot of people thought back then that this brilliant and youthful leader of the Cincinnati Archdiocese would be the first American pope. and nobody was surprised when he was named a cardinal and went to Chicago. While he was there, he did precisely what might be expected of a great man who is also good.

I wish I had the chance to sit next to him again at dinner. This time, I think I would like to say some things. I wonder if he knew how important he was to the spiritual life of people who are Presbyterian and Methodist and Baptist. Do you suppose he realized what a stunning example of goodness he was to us sinners of all persuasions?

In a world filled with leaders — religious and otherwise — who say one thing and mean another, Cardinal Bernardin has always told the truth. Always. He attacked racism, calling it worse than sin. He condemned the bombing of abortion clinics. He insisted that the Catholic church face the problem of sexual abuse by priests.

It must have been unendurable that he himself was accused of such a crime. In nineteen ninety-three, a former seminarian said Cardinal Bernardin had molested him in the nineteen seventies. It was all very public and very ugly. And very untrue.

Steven Cook recanted his accusation against Cardinal Bernardin, who ordered his lawyers not to retaliate with countersuits. The cardinal said he didn't want victims of genuine abuse to be afraid to come forward. Suffering from AIDS, Mr. Cook died. But not before Cardinal Bernardin, this "prince of the church," flew to Philadelphia to meet with him. I do not believe that this was for any sort of "closure" for Cardinal Bernardin. I think he was flying to the rescue of a lost soul.

Cardinal Bernardin allowed the dying man to say he was sorry and forgave him promptly and absolutely. He celebrated Mass and gave Steven Cook a Bible. "In every family, there are times when there is hurt, anger, alienation. But we cannot run away from our family. We have only one family, so we must make every effort to be reconciled," the cardinal said.

And once again, this great and good man reminds us that sometimes we worry about all the wrong things.

— *October, 1996*

Two

HEALTHY COMPLAINTS, INCLUDING MY FORMER BREAST

---

*"There are a lot of things
worse than dying, and being
afraid all the time would be
one of them."*
—*Cancer survivor*

SOMEBODY I LIKE said to me, "Uh, do you think you could write about breast cancer? Uh, your breast cancer?" Well, of course I could. Haven't I stood up in front of auditoriums full of strangers to talk about it? Once, at the request of the governor's wife, I even talked about it on the public square at noon.

You can imagine how much fun that was. Particularly for the audience. Picture a bunch of innocent people eating fat-free yogurt and minding their own business when, all of a sudden, some woman behind a microphone starts talking about her former breast, right in front of God and the governor's wife and assorted pigeons.

So, if I could do that, it would be a breeze to talk about it with my own personal readers, who can turn the page if they want. It is, in fact, a duty. Since I was lucky enough to discover that I had breast cancer, my assignment, as I understand it, is to show up everywhere I can for the rest of my life looking as healthy as possible. When I say lucky, of course, I mean that I was lucky to discover cancer, not to get it. And I was lucky I had a garden-variety breast cancer, found early, during a routine mammogram. I'm lucky I'm not poor.

Although it is an adventure I would rather have missed, it really hasn't been as awful as I thought it might be. I have been surprised at the good things that have happened. For instance, there's a little window of opportunity, right around the time you have been diagnosed or maybe when you're having chemo, when people will forgive you anything.

That's the time to get the tattoo you've always wanted. Park in somebody else's parking space. Buy retail. Go through the express lane at the grocery store with thirteen items. You can use it selectively. I read somewhere that after you have had breast cancer, you can never, ever operate a vacuum cleaner again. And I'm also sure it's dangerous for me to clean bathrooms. However, tennis and horseback riding are good therapy.

I don't keep anything that is fancy enough to be called a journal or a diary, but I do write notes to myself in a calendar I keep. I looked back to some notes I made when I was diagnosed with cancer.

I clipped a newspaper story that said that breast cancer afflicts one in nine women. I wrote: "I can find a great silver lining here. I will consider that I have protected eight other women. I hope they are all poor and have no medical insurance."

And another entry: "There are a lot of things worse than dying. And being afraid would be one of them."

Cancer has cured me of many things. I believe it has cured me of worrying about things that don't matter. Wrinkles? So what? Cellulite? Who cares? Cancer has cured me of putting things off until later. Good things, that is. I still put off writing thank-you notes and starting on a real exercise program or yard work.

However, I would not recommend it to my friends.

I saw a photo exhibit not long ago called "The Face of Breast Cancer," a touching tribute to women from every state in the union who have died from breast cancer. There was also a "Survivor's Wall." I remember noticing how happy these women looked. Some of them probably have been told they have a good attitude. Some people say it with the implication that you can sort of think your way back to health.

I can tell you that I took my good attitude right over to Pill Hill, where I got every bit of surgery and drugs they'd give me. I take two pills every day and see two doctors six times a year. I have a mammogram once a year and hold my breath until they tell me the results.

I'm not complaining, really I'm not. After all, I'm here to tell the story.

— November, 1995

THE SMARTEST KIDS IN THE CLASS

HERE'S WHAT I'D like to do: I'd like to put all the doctors in this country in a big drafty auditorium. They would be wearing paper robes, equally drafty. Here's what I'd say.

Isn't it about time you rescue medicine from the questionable mercies of business and politics? You were the smartest kids in the class. So why are you letting everybody else tell you how to do your jobs?

We all know dimwits who became journalists and lawyers and insurance executives. But I can't think of a single instance when somebody said, "Geez, did you hear that Buzzy Binkley became a doctor? I always thought he was a little slow."

You people who became doctors were the brains, the bookworms, the Merit Scholars, the Eagle Scouts, the hall monitors. You were the ones whose homework the rest of us copied. Because you had the answers. You are the people with the magnificent arrogance to put your hands around a pulsing human heart. You are the voices brave enough to give the bad news.

So, what's the problem? Are you scared of a bunch of bean counters? You whipped their butts on the SATs. And now they're making medical decisions "in consultation" with you. Consultation? Why aren't you running the show? Are you really prepared to become just another employee?

Why have you allowed insurance companies and managed care to demand that young couples leave the car running when they enter the maternity ward? Where have you been? On some extended golf holiday? Have you sent your best and brightest out to do battle, attend the meetings, work on the committees?

Is it the money? Is it us? Are you tired of taking care of us? And our untidy illnesses? Does it honk you off that Shaquille O'Neal is going to get one hundred twenty million dollars to dunk round balls and you still owe money on your medical-school loans?

I beg of you. Get back in the game. When I get sick, I'd still like to know there's a doctor in charge. Not some MBA. I sure don't want Hillary Clinton or Newt Gingrich or Ted Kennedy to be taking my temperature.

Okay. Now take off those ridiculous paper robes and get out there and start acting like doctors again.

— *National Public Radio,*
August, 1996

THE BRAIN IS A TERRIBLE THING TO WASTE

EVERY TIME THEY come up with something new that isn't good for you, it is something I especially like. Don't smoke. Don't eat cheese. Don't eat eggs unless you cook them at nine hundred forty degrees for four days. Don't sit in the sun. Don't sit on the couch. In fact, don't sit down at all, except to floss your teeth. Don't have wild, erotic, promiscuous sex unless vicariously on daytime television.

Don't. Don't. Don't.

This is why I was so enthusiastic about a new report warning people not to eat squirrel brains. This is a diet hardship I feel prepared to endure. In addition to squirrel brains, doctors have issued a warning that we should all curb our desires for the brains of elk, deer, mink and rodents. I am thinking of giving them all up for Lent.

Squirrels, according to a study by the neurology department at the University of Kentucky in Lexington, might carry a variant of mad cow disease. In the last four years, eleven people in rural Kentucky have contracted this rare disease.

"All of them were squirrel-brain eaters," one of the doctors said.

Well, I don't have to be hit over the head with a brick. Beginning right this minute, I am swearing off squirrel brains for good. If I find myself about to fall off the squirrel-brain wagon, I will distract myself with chocolate mint chip ice cream. Or Nacho Cheese Doritos, which have so far not been part of any official warning.

The next time I'm wondering whether I should climb on the treadmill for an hour, I'll notice that I haven't been eating any squirrel brains. While I'm filled with self-loathing after a popcorn hog-arama, I'll remind myself that somewhere in Kentucky, people who have no regard for their health are gorging on you-know-what.

You'd think learning that you're not supposed to do something you didn't want to do in the first place would be about all the good news a person could get in one week. But, as it happens, my personal cup runneth over. After years of filling out *Reader's Digest* sweepstakes forms and licking Publisher's Clearinghouse stamps, I received notice of a prize I would be delighted not to win.

First of all, you have to go to an exhibit of the art of Yoko Ono. To give you an idea of what that might be like, you should know that part of it is an interactive work, "Cleaning

Piece," which instructs visitors to move river stones from one pile to another, "assigning emotions to the rocks such as sorrow and happiness."

Also on display is something called "Telephone Peace," which includes an actual telephone, promising the occasional call from the artist herself. She didn't say when or how often she'd call, and one exhibitor said "you just have to be lucky enough to be standing next to the exhibit when the phone rings."

I didn't know how to break it to her, but most people's idea of luck is Ed McMahon showing up on Super Bowl Sunday with a check for a million dollars. And I'd rather move around a big rock representing sorrow than chat with Yoko Ono. What would I say?

"Uh. Hi, Yoko. Howzit going? Say, I don't mean to be rude, but why did you ruin the Beatles? Also, why were you always taking off your clothes?

Then, no doubt, somebody would wrest the phone from me and hand me a rock that represents being a big embarrassment to my hometown, my country, and possibly the planet. I hope they'd give me one more chance to say something important and meaningful.

"Yo, Yoko. Peace. Love. And don't eat any squirrel brains.

— *September, 1997*

24

WHEN THE WORLD WAS OUR ASHTRAY

HELLO? COUGH. COUGH. Are you there? My eyes are watering, and I can't see too well. Whew. This place smells terrible. Do you think it's the smoke? Well, maybe you're right. It could just be the Dumpster we're leaning on. It's getting harder and harder to find someplace to relax and have a cigarette. Remember when you could smoke anywhere?

Boy, those were the days. The world was our ashtray. We could smoke in department stores, on airplanes, in doctors' offices. Remember those little ashtrays on stands? You hardly ever see those anymore. We used to be allowed to smoke in hospitals, for Pete's sake, as long as we didn't light up next to somebody in an oxygen tent.

We could lean back after dinner in any fine restaurant and puff away anytime we pleased. If there was no ashtray on the table, it was an oversight. The really good restaurants had waiters who prided themselves on being able to light your cigarette before you could put it to your lips.

When other diners complained that they couldn't taste their food over the aroma of your Winston, well, they were just poor sports and weenies. What we did with our own, personal lungs was none of their business. Sometimes people would actually refuse to let us exercise our God-given right to blow nicotine and carbon monoxide all over the planet.

Unless they were in an iron lung, we insisted on a darn good excuse. For instance, "I'm allergic." And they'd better have the hives to prove it.

If, for some inexplicable reason, we weren't allowed to smoke at work, the company would thoughtfully — and apologetically — provide a smokers' lounge. Chairs, tables, ashtrays. It was splendid, really, especially by today's standards.

My fellow buttheads, those days are long gone. The only reminders we have of a world when everybody was expected to smoke is the automatic inclusion of ashtrays and lighters in our automobiles. Well, that and all the lung cancer, heart disease and emphysema. Although the poor, ignorant tobacco companies find themselves mostly still unconvinced that their product is lethal, the rest of us know the truth. Cigarettes were killing us. Worse, they were killing the people around us.

The turnaround has been absolutely amazing. Now maybe we can rethink alcohol and guns. Even the most avid anti-smokers (we buttheads like to refer to them as the smugheads) would have to admit that nobody ever smoked her brains out, then climbed into a car and killed somebody, or had a little too much to smoke and then beat the living hell out of his wife.

But tobacco's days as an unregulated vice are numbered. Think of it, ordinary cigarettes could become illegal, forbidden fruit, a wonderful new lure for teen-agers, who already are getting hooked in record numbers. I'm sure the marketing departments of RJR Nabisco, *et al* will be alert to this opportunity.

A controlled substance with an illegal jolly Joe Camel as pusher. This would click with a whole new generation. It's thrilling. They'll love it. In fact, it will take their breath away.

— *May, 1996*

THE NO-SWEAT DIET PLAN

THIS COULD BE the answer to our prayers, my fellow food lovers and aerobics haters. Men in white lab coats are talking again about an anti-fat pill, an easy way to be thin and trim. Scientists in California say they have discovered a gene that could lead to a drug that helps people get rid of "unwanted flab."

These guys have been spending too much time around test tubes. Don't they know that all flab is unwanted? And that we are willing to try anything (short of eating sensibly and exercising) to get rid of it? Haven't we signed up to be liposuctioned and fen-phened? Haven't we faithfully purchased the Buns of Steel video? Haven't we worshipped at the altars of Jenny Craig and Oprah? Haven't we Weight Watched?

Haven't we eaten enough fiber to insulate a house? Haven't we tried the Grapefruit Diet and the Scarsdale Diet and the Hollywood Diet? (Sometimes all three simultaneously, if we were coming up on a high school reunion.) Haven't we counted fat grams? Haven't we tried to substitute fat-free yogurt on dishes that beg for sour cream?

Does anybody think we were all excited about olestra because we thought we might enjoy anal leakage? Is there any other conceivable reason that we would listen to anything at all that Suzanne Somers has to say or to sell?

These same scientists say their discovery might also explain why some people are prone to weight gain. That's probably important information, but just not as interesting as the other aspects of their research. We already have affixed the blame to our mothers, to menopause, to our fathers, to stress, to our thyroids, to the holidays, to salt, to Sara Lee.

We are very good at deciding why blubber is not our fault. Now all we need is an easy, fool-proof, temptation-proof way to get rid of it. The last word we had from the laboratory was that yo-yo dieting was bad for us. Imagine that. You gain and lose the same fifteen pounds three or four times over the space of six months and that's not good for you.

We are shocked, *shocked*. We overeat, we diet, we lose. Then we celebrate by going out to dinner. And we gain it all back again, in half the time it took us to lose the extra poundage. The unfairness of this has been discussed over many a meal that includes almost no fat whatsoever, unless you count the fried cheese appetizers somebody else ordered or the shared dessert.

And everyone knows that neither of these things counts, nor does any calorie consumed standing up at cocktail parties or hanging over a sink.

Some scientists are working on a drug that would help the body burn off more calories, rather than store them as fat. They say a person might be able to lose five pounds a year with every one-tenth of a degree increase in body temperature. That doesn't sound like much to me. For men, it would be about like letting a woman set the thermostat in their homes during the winter.

What's a little heat? Especially if you don't have to really sweat. A tenth of a degree is nothing. It's not like you have to spend an hour on a Stairmaster or a stationary bike. If the drug companies give us this magic pill, we'll be able to concentrate on other things we'd like to improve. Such as wrinkles. Or baldness. Or even our minds.

— *March, 1997*

Three

MOTHERS AND

OTHER HEROES

> *"I could always go home*
> *and be wonderful, even if*
> *I stunk everyplace else."*
> —*Jan Annett, teacher*

A ROUND OF APPLAUSE
FOR THE BLEACHERS

THANKS TO MY mother, I will never be famous.

While Joan Crawford was beating her daughter with wire clothes hangers, my Mommie Dearest was signing up to be a Girl Scout Brownie leader. Therefore, Christina Crawford had the opportunity to be a best-selling author and talk show guest. I learned how to tie a square knot and sing "Do your ears hang low" in a three-part round.

So far, this has not qualified me to be a guest on Oprah.

Mom never abused me, although she did make me go to school on the Queen Mother of all bad hair days — right after a Toni home permanent. And she had some terrible, awful, old-fashioned rules. She would not let me shave my legs until I was in the sixth grade, and I was not allowed to wear a bra until I actually needed one.

"What about a training bra?" I wailed desperately.

"It depends," my mother said darkly, "on what you will be training them to do."

Some mothers taught their daughters how to be men traps: "Never beat him at any sport, Dear." That was not my mother's way. Instead, she told my brothers that they had to let me play baseball with them and made my brother Steve show me how to throw a spiral pass. She told me I should play to win, even if my opponent was one of the few boys in the seventh grade who was taller than I.

Thanks to my mother, I had to settle for brainy boys who didn't mind if you were smart and beat them at tennis. I can probably blame her for the fact that I married a man who is bright and secure. And, for that, he can probably blame his mother. A wonderful cook, she headed for the kitchen after a full day of bouncing around on a tractor or some other big, incomprehensible machine that cultivates the modern farm.

Her garden was both beautiful and bountiful, and she "put up" what they couldn't eat right away and gave it to families who did not have gardens. Or good cooks. She devoted her life to making a home for her husband and two sons. But she never made me feel guilty because I "worked outside the home," and she never played politics with holidays.

At her funeral, people we didn't know came forward to say how much they loved her. I hope they told her. I wish I had.

"Happy families are all alike; every unhappy family is unhappy in its own way," according to Tolstoy. Maybe that's why somebody else's good mom sounds familiar. My friend, Jan, says that, thanks to her mother, "I could always go home and be wonderful, even if I stunk everywhere else."

That about sums it up.

There are some terrible mothers in this world. Just this minute, let's ignore them and think about our moms instead — yours and mine. Let's celebrate the mom who let you get a dog even though she knew you wouldn't really be the one to feed and walk it. The mom who ruined her eyes making your prom dress. The mom who stayed up all night with you to finish your science project. The mom who thought you were the bravest and handsomest boy on the team. The smartest girl in your class. The best one. And you knew that she thought so. And still does.

Our mothers, of course, are wonderfully unique. But they are the same in that one way. If you do not believe me, picture your own mother's face the last time you surprised her with a visit or maybe after you hadn't seen her for a while. Remember how she looked when she caught sight of you. Just then, didn't you feel, well, kind of famous? Thanks to your mother.

—*May, 1997*

GRANDMA'S HANDS

MATTIE JOHNSON WOULD just like to teach some of the girls to sew. It is something she can do, and there's nothing wrong with starting small. Even though the problems seem so big. "You know what I'm saying? Drugs, guns." She rolls her eyes.

Her friend Barbara's grown son was murdered — right in front of hundreds of children at a peace rally at his high school. And the girls, well, they are having babies. Too many babies. "They don't know anything about how to take care of them. It worries me."

I have found Mattie in the basement of an apartment building in one of the poorest parts of the city. Following instructions, I go to the side of the building and down a short flight of steps to a metal door.

A neatly lettered sign says, "Grandma's Hands. We are selling in the basement." A list of what they're selling — pop, candy, hot dogs, pickles — and their prices, considerably below market, in my opinion.

Another piece of paper, taped to the door, advises, "KNOCK HARD." So I do.

Luckily, I have arrived before the rush, before school lets out. Therefore, I have the more-or-less undivided attention of Mattie Johnson, head grandma. This is the basement of one of twenty-six buildings that make up Cincinnati's largest public housing development.

It is warm, neat as a pin and smells of freshly popped popcorn. It feels the way my house felt when I got home from school. A study room is empty right now, waiting for Lottie Thomas, who tutors twenty-five to thirty kids every afternoon. There's also a recreation room with a television. Next to that is storage for Mattie's creations: aprons, fabric tote bags, stuffed animals.

The aprons are brightly colored with bib tops and big, honest pockets. The handles of the bags are reinforced. Everything is carefully finished, mostly by machine, but with some hand work. Most items are two or three dollars. It doesn't seem like enough, but I'm not ashamed to say I bought as much as I could carry. It was fine work, and I wish I'd been there for the quilt sale.

Mattie and her five friends, the rest of the grandma crew, have come to believe that they have some skills to pass along. Among them, they've got maybe four hundred years of experience. Besides, "When you're sitting around sewing and cooking, that's when a lot of talking gets done."

By now, the kids are out of school.

"You come here, Handsome, and give me my hug."

"What did you make? Let me see. Oh, you can draw so good."

"Where are your gloves?"

"Now don't you talk smart to me."

"You got homework?"

Grandmas. A warmth of them. Six. They sell things to raise money because otherwise, "Every time you need something you have to go ask The Man." They are not looking for handouts.

Next to the kitchen is a photo of Mattie. "I am looking good," she laughs, "don't you think?" I do. More black than gray in the curls below her black ball cap. Smooth face, laugh lines only. She just turned seventy. She says she has reared twenty children, in mostly informal arrangements. She and her late husband, James, had none of their own.

After Hodgkin's disease and colon cancer, "I'm still here, so I guess God is leaving me to do something for somebody."

Six old women. They are experts in the art of cooking

and sewing and grand masters in the art of hugging and scolding. They can silence a smart mouth at ten paces and spot a missing button at twenty.

Grandmas, every one of them.

They are selling in the basement. And they are giving something you can't buy.

— November, 1996

A SMALL MEMORY LAPSE

I WONDER WHY, if I'm so bad at names, I can still remember every one of my grade school teachers.

Mrs. Winegardner, grade one. Lilac perfume and sensible shoes. Carried a pitch pipe and once scraped the mud off my shoes with a popsicle stick when I said my dear, gentle mother would kill me when she saw them.

Mrs. Boger, grade two. Red lipstick, red hair and a red suit with a white blouse. Every day. She was what was known as strict. Nobody ever had the guts to find out what she'd do if you got caught chewing gum, but we were pretty sure it was something like three days in the electric chair.

Miss Koffel, grade three. She broke all the rules. We had a pet show with live animals and took thirteen field trips. She spent recesses with the slow learner who later went to Stanford. She showed us how to make ice cream out of snow. She convinced us we were valuable and admirable. Her garters sagged, her hair was tousled and she had a wart on her chin. We thought she was gorgeous.

Mrs. Watkins, grade four. Curly blond hair, a dazzling smile, didn't assign homework. Lots of hugs and pats on the head. Her specialty was geography. I still believe Egypt is adjacent to Bolivia.

Miss Spur, grade five. Impressively proportioned backside, wire spectacles, pursed lips. She made fun of stuttering and shabby clothes and fawned on the doctor's daughter. Absenteeism was rampant, and if we hadn't been ten years old we would have been alcoholic as well.

Mrs. Core, grade six. Beautiful jewelry. Actually laughed right out loud, right in front of us. Read to us every day from good books. We were allowed to get a drink of water or go to the rest room without asking. Spoke softly and drove a big car.

See what I mean? Why do I have trouble remembering the name of the guy who was President right before Jimmy Carter? I do remember that his wife had a facelift and said it would be okay for their daughter to have premarital sex and that he smoked a pipe (which he couldn't do and walk at the same time). I guess only the really important stuff stays with me.

Those of us with kids are acutely aware of our influence of them. We secretly fear that if we make one wrong move, they're going to purchase a rifle on their eighteenth birthday and climb to the top of a tower. And we're painfully aware of peer pressure. If they sit next to the wrong person in eighth-period study hall, we're afraid they will forget everything we have told them and they will follow their new friend to the Gates of Hell. Or to a shopping mall.

But, really, what about the people who have their attention five or six hours a day during their most impressionable years? What of grade school teachers and how they made us feel about ourselves and the start they gave us? When it comes time for teacher conferences and school levies and how much we're willing to spend on education, it seems to me that these are things worth remembering.

— *WVXU radio, October, 1992*

Oklahoma Looks A Lot Like Home

THIS IS ABOUT Oklahoma City, I promise, but I want to get there through the flat farmlands of Ohio.

When my husband and I were first married, we went to his mom and dad's house for Sunday dinner. At noon. Supper was at night, and lunch was not something they ate, but something for those people who "slept in" until six.

After a relentlessly bountiful farm meal — two kinds of meat and mashed potatoes and gravy and noodles and green beans with ham and made-from-scratch pie — my pants fit like a tourniquet, and I wondered whether it would be impolite to lapse into a coma. My father-in-law had disappeared toward the barn, where I thought maybe he'd hidden a six-pack of Maalox.

Instead, he drove down the lane on a green John Deere tractor and waited at the edge of the road. I looked out the window to see a dozen dusty farm machines rumbling toward us. My mother-in-law told me a neighbor was sick and unable to harvest his crop — actually she said "take off his beans," but I knew what she meant.

"That is," I said fatuously, "so nice."

She looked at me as though I was from Mars. "Well, what else would we do?"

What else, indeed.

You could have ignored them or ripped them off. You could have pretended not to notice. You could have demanded that a government agency step in. You could have insisted on a day of rest after six days of working your own fields.

And the people of Oklahoma City might have behaved very differently after the Alfred P. Murrah Federal Building was blasted by a 4,800-pound truck bomb on April 19, 1995. The might have looted. But of course, they did not. Not once. Not ever. They lined up to give blood, and collected bedsheets and tarps to serve as makeshift bodybags.

Volunteers crawled through a treachery of collapsed walls and dangling wires and sagging floors, over bodies and parts of bodies, looking for life. A firefighter said, "All I've found here is a baby's finger and an American flag. You find out who did this."

After Timothy McVeigh was found guilty, they could have mobbed him. They could have sent threatening letters to his court-appointed attorney. Most of them were disappointed, some angry, when the trial was moved to Denver. They could have rioted.

What they did instead was raise seven million dollars for scholarships for the seventy children orphaned and one hundred twenty who lost one parent. They paid for the funerals of strangers. They were at the bedsides of survivors, twenty-nine of whom are permanently disfigured. They planted trees. They prayed. They left teddy bears and flowers at the base of the rubble. A slippery elm, scarred from the blast, became their survival symbol.

Oklahoma Gov. Frank Keating said firmly, "Anyone who would murder one hundred sixty-eight of his neighbors and smash into oblivion nineteen children deserves the death penalty."

That sounds about right, too. These people have been dignified and generous, but they are also strong and tough. Farmers keep nice big dogs that flop lazily on the porch, letting barn kittens tumble over their paws. But they will use their teeth on intruders.

Straddling an oil field and boasting the national Cowboy Hall of Fame, Oklahoma City was settled in a single day in April, eighteen eighty-nine, when ten thousand homestead-

ers charged in to stake the first claim. Tough guys and farmers. Now its citizens make more money from industry than
from the land, but they still grow respectable crops of winter
wheat, sorghum and soybeans.

Not quite Texas, a little bit Sunbelt, a shade Midwestern,
Oklahoma is our country's heartland. We know its people.
They are like all of us. On a good day.

In the midst of the trial, a chirpy network subanchor was
talking to a man from Oklahoma City about the way the town
has rallied behind the victims. As she blithered — fatuously
— about the remarkable kindness and grace of the people of
Oklahoma, the look on the man's face was very familiar. It
was the "you must be from Mars" face, and I thought I knew
what he was thinking.

"What else would we do?"

— *June, 1997*

FAMILY VALUES PUT
TO THE TEST

WE HEAR A LOT about family values from people who
wouldn't know a family if they fell over one having Thanksgiving dinner. They should meet the Nolans.

Seven kids, they scattered in at least that many direc-
tions during the day. They always reassembled at dinnertime.

It was a rule. Unbreakable.

They identify their Price Hill neighborhood, as west-siders will, by their parish. Everybody went to St. William, every morning.

St.Patrick's Day was big, bigger than Christmas. Ed Nolan would buy green bread from nearby St. Lawrence Bakery. And every kid got a new green outfit.

A close family even after Ed died in nineteen seventy-two, Tim, Dan and Terry subbed for their dad at father-daughter banquets and soccer. The older kids helped with the younger ones, and Ed, who had been a vice president at Heekin Can Company, left Phyllis fixed well enough to stay at home.

"When Mom was little, she hated coming home to an empty house," Dan says, "so we never did. She was always in the kitchen when we got home from school."

Dan — who is actually Brother Dan, a Franciscan friar — says right after his father died, he heard his mother say, "Lord, I think I can handle this, but please don't take one of my kids before me." That, she thought she could not handle.

But she did.

Her son Terry Nolan died just two weeks shy of his forty-ninth birthday. Bright, funny, handsome Terry Nolan. Kate Nolan, who works for the Legal Aid Society, says she probably has her brother to thank for making it through high school.

He forged her parents' signatures on demerit cards sent home by the nuns from Seton High School. Okay, so he wasn't a saint. But he sure was a nice guy. "Everyone loved Terry," Kate says.

They still do.

Phyllis, seventy-six, and her entire brood marched ten kilometers in his honor. In fact, there were about twenty family members, including nieces and nephews. The youngest was two and traveled in a wagon. Phyllis, plagued by arthritis, rode in a wheelchair. The Nolans collected about one thousand dollars for AIDS Volunteers of Cincinnati.

Yes, Terry Nolan died of AIDS. And yes, he was gay, in case you were wondering.

It was never a secret in the Nolan family, and they spoke of Terry's illness openly to their friends, almost from the beginning. Terry was diagnosed in nineteen eighty-eight, just before he moved to Miami with his partner of twenty-four years, Dann Schultz.

The Nolans rallied. Big surprise, right? After you spend about two minutes with any of them, you can't imagine they'd do anything else.

Kate, who flew to Florida fifteen times last year, has enough frequent flier miles and peanuts to open her own airline. Danny, who's not seven and lives in Muncie, Indiana, called his uncle every time he was allowed. Which was all the time.

"The little ones, I think, kept him alive," Dan says. "He wanted as much time, as many memories, as he could manage." After one of his sisters had her baby, Dan joked, "Quick. somebody get pregnant. Give him something more to live for."

But no matter how strong your resolve, how loving your family, how devout your prayers, this is one disease that eventually kills you.

Terry went down the aisle of St. William Church one last time, carried by his six brothers and sisters. Phyllis, stronger all along than anybody thought she'd be, walked behind her son's casket with Dann Schultz. Dann read a letter from Terry. Typically, Terry tried to console them: "My forty-eight years of this life have been wonderful."

The Terry Nolan Walking Team wore T-shirts in "Caribbean blue," Terry's favorite color. They were noisy and, as usual, had a pretty good time.

But they never forgot why they were there.

— *September, 1996*

Four

SEXUAL POLITICS
MAKE STRANGE
BEDFELLOWS

"Shoot me."
—*Overheard during the*
discomfort of childbirth.

WINNING BY A HAIR

NEXT TO SPEEDO bathing suits, what women in America find most unattractive in a man is hair sculpture. Men, you should know that a good, honest bald head or even a toupee beats a few tortured strands trying to do the work of an entire head of hair. The dreaded combovers. When a guy's part gets lower and lower and the hair on that side gets longer and longer until there's enough to plaster across the top of his head.

This is particularly damaging for politicians. Would you really trust a man who thinks you're so dumb you don't notice that the hair on the top of his head is rooted just above his ear? And what about parades? Sitting on the back of a convertible? Unless he resorts to Crazy Glue, he's going to have to wave with one hand and hold his hair down with the other.

Rudy Guiliani lost his first bid to be mayor of New York City when a photographer captured a breeze lifting Mr. Juliani's comb-over about four inches over his head. He gave up the foot-long strands, joined the hair club and is now mayor of New York City.

The people have spoken. We do not want a person in a position of power who might be under the influence of Dippity Doo fumes or who suffers from mousse abuse. Or who looks silly. We will elect people who are mean. We will elect people who are drunks and philanderers. We will even elect people who are stupid. We seem to adore electing people who are crooked. But we will never elect anybody who is laughable. Gerald Ford tripped once too often. And the beginning of the end for George Bush, if you ask me, was when he barfed on the Japanese premier.

I mention this only because I think they're planning to hold an election again next year, then before you know it, we'll be deep in the Really Big One, where we decide who's going to be running around the White House in jogging shorts. Anyway, I have seen a shocking number of combovers on both sides of the aisle, so I implore you.

Guys, act now. Before it's too late. Public office is too important to let the decision turn on a hair.

— *National Public Radio,*
December, 1992

BUSINESS IS NOW
OFFICIALLY WOMEN'S WORK

THAT WAS NOT a cold front we just experienced, Cincinnati gentlepersons. The chill you felt was hell freezing over.

The Commercial Club now has three female members.

If you've never heard of the Commercial Club, that has always been just fine with its members. They're not what you might call publicity hounds. For one hundred sixteen years, these movers and shakers have been quietly slipping into boiled shirts and dinner jackets for meetings at the institutionally stuffy Queen City Club.

Membership is noted publicly only in their obituaries, listing civic and social ties: Yale Club, Queen City Club, Camargo, the Literary Club. And the Commercial Club.

It has always been a status symbol for people who already had status to burn.

According to its constitution, the club's purpose is to "promote the commercial, industrial and cultural interests of Cincinnati and environs, by social intercourse, the exchange of views and other such activities." Civilized and benign. And exclusive. Very exclusive.

"Clubs" like this one have nothing to do with socializing and everything to do with getting things done. With power.

Imagine how much easier it is if you have an idea for, say, a pair of new stadiums to simply pick up the phone to call the guy who shared the Huitres de Chesapeake with you the week before. Or if you want to find a new law firm or portfolio manager, well, it is always more comfortable to deal with somebody who just sat in the same golf cart.

We women have known this for as long as we've been working, as they say, "outside the home." And we have had some misguided ideas about what to do. One woman I know believed she could golf her way to the top. She said a lot of business is transacted on the links, so she started taking golf lessons.

"Patty," I asked, "do you think your boss hasn't asked you to join his foursome because he's afraid you won't keep your head down and your elbows in? Do you think you haven't been invited to join the Queen City Club because they're afraid you don't know how to eat?"

Several years ago, some executives tried to start a rival club, just for women. Somebody noticed that we weren't going to get any more prosperous by hanging around with each other. Our solution was to do nothing, except complain bitterly every chance we got.

And, of course, we continued to work hard, hoping to get ahead.

The trio who broke the gender barrier are all CEOs. Accomplished women, they have volunteered for good causes and have made significant contributions not only to their companies, but to the community. Would it be churlish to notice that it's about time they joined the club? Would it be unladylike to wonder what took so long? Is it impolite to point out that the world did not come to an end because three women have been allowed to sit at the table?

Do you suppose that the old guard would be offended if I mentioned that they are lucky to have these women as members? Not the other way around.

The club secretary says there's no particular reason the club decided to admit women this year. And it's true that the club wasn't being picketed or sued. We haven't even complained much lately.

But I'd like to think that there were a lot of particular reasons why these good citizens and decent fellows stepped belatedly into the real world. I'd like to think that they have noticed the contributions made to their companies by female executives.

I'd like to think that they were embarrassed for the women they respect to know they belonged to a club that would not permit female members. I'd like to think that some of the members have daughters, whom they admire, whom they consider to be first-class citizens, smart and capable. As good as any man.

At least that is what I would like to think.

— *June, 1996*

WE CAN SEE THE GLASS CEILING

A BIG IMPORTANT Labor Department study says men get ninety-five percent of the fancy jobs in this country. Trust me. One hundred percent of America's women already knew this.

We just didn't know what to do about it. We tried dressing like men and that didn't work. We've been farming our kids out to day care centers and our liberated husbands have been doing the laundry and we've been networking like banshees. But the white guys still have the corner offices.

When my husband and I went to natural childbirth classes before our daughter was born, the instructor used to talk about the "discomfort" of childbirth. Now, to me, "discomfort" means something like sitting on a wrinkle in my skirt. I did not think that this word was a fair description of my experiences in the labor room.

I was very happy when the doctor said it was time for my anesthetic and proud that I did not, as did my friend Joyce, ask the doctors to shoot me.

Thirteen years later, I felt the same way about the "discomfort" of having a teenager. For those of you who have a child twelve or younger, I don't want to be the bearer of bad tidings, but my friend Joyce has begun to beg people to shoot her again.

But no matter how many of my sweaters disappear into the Bermuda Triangle that is my daughter's bedroom, no matter how often I worry that MTV will turn her brain to shushi, I am crazy about her. And I took it for granted that my generation was doing the spadework for her.

We've waited patiently in line for three decades. We've gone to good schools and worked late hours. We've learned to smoke and have heart attacks and ulcers. We even know how to play golf.

Now we just have to explain to our daughters about the "discomfort" of banging your head against a brick wall — and a glass ceiling.

—*National Public Radio,*
March, 1995

COULDN'T ANYBODY
SAVE THIS CHILD?

THIS IS NOT about a murdering mother.

It's about the dad.

Back in July, people in Dayton, Ohio, were looking for Samantha Ritchie, four years old, last seen wearing a pink nightgown. Three feet tall, about thirty pounds.

Her mother, Therressa Jolynn Ritchie, pleaded for the child's return. Samantha's photograph was all over the newspapers and television. A baby's face. Blonde pigtails. Wide mouth in a narrow smile. Almond-shaped brown eyes looking right into the cameras. You probably saw the picture.

If you did, you know what happened.

Searchers found the little body, pinned by scrap metal and chunks of cement, in a watery pit about a block from her home. Jolynn was convicted of the murder. Police say "Sam" stumbled upon her mother having sex with a neighbor. Having already demonstrated the morals of a mink, this neighbor testified that he stood there holding his pants while Jolynn clubbed the child to death.

Another neighbor, a woman, shut her door in this baby's face at one-thirty in the morning. Three years ago, the Children Services Board investigated complaints that Jolynn Ritchie's children — Samantha and three older half-brothers — were not being properly supervised.

"They checked it out and determined there was nothing there," said a spokesperson. "We never heard anything further."

Geez. Maybe the kids lost your phone number. Where were the neighbors and family? The media? Where was any of us? Didn't anybody see anything that would have caused him to get involved?

And where was this child's father?

You don't hear much about him. From the beginning, he stoutly refused to be part of a circus. While some volunteers were "scheduling interviews" and his former wife drank with an old boyfriend named Junebug, Denton Ritchie was looking for his daughter.

He collapsed two days after she was reported missing. He had not eaten or slept. He told a friend maybe when Samantha was found he could finally get custody. You've heard about deadbeat dads? This guy wasn't one of them. He drives a garbage truck for the city of Dayton, and he never missed a three hundred thirteen dollar monthly support payment for Samantha, his only child.

Already divorced twice, he married Samantha's mother in nineteen ninety, about a month before he was sent to the Persian Gulf. A sergeant in the Army Reserve, Denton Ritchie, thirty-four, returned home to find a wife who was using crack cocaine. He told her he wanted a divorce. And his child.

Montgomery County Domestic Relations Court records show that Denton Ritchie petitioned for custody on May tenth, nineteen ninety-five. He claimed his daughter was abducted to Kentucky for two years. Jolynn Ritchie said she moved there to get her life in order. I don't know. But I do know that about a year before Samantha's murder, her mother tangled with the law and was convicted of assault. I know she lived in unspeakable filth.

I don't know what the problem with Denton Ritchie was. Being a man, I guess. Anyway, the court awarded custody of Samantha to her mother on July eleventh, nineteen ninety-five. Seven days before she was murdered.

A small man, not much over five feet tall, Denton Ritchie was in court every single day of the murder trial. Except when they showed the autopsy pictures. When attorneys made final arguments in a courtroom awash in leather and long greasy hair, Denton Ritchie's hair was closely cropped and his suit brown wool. Jolynn Ritchie, twenty-five, flirted and joked with deputies before the verdict.

She saw me gaping at her and smiled pleasantly, looking like a chunky kid in detention. No makeup and a pimple northwest of her mouth. Neatly pressed pink blouse under a gray jumper. She didn't cry a single tear or flinch once. Not even when the prosecutor described Samantha's last moments.

Across the room, Denton Ritchie put his head in his hands and cried as though his heart would break.

— *February, 1996*

The View From The Citadel

WATCHING THOSE BOYS at the Citadel dancing in the rain after Shannon Faulkner washed out didn't make me wonder how she could have quit in less than a week. It makes me wonder instead how she managed to go to class with these guys for more than a year. It also makes me wonder why adults at that school think that what these potential men need is more of each other.

Ms. Faulkner, for those who are not students of almost-current events, was the first female to be admitted to the Citadel military school. She was accepted in nineteen ninety-three after references to her sex were deleted from her high school transcript. When the school found out she was a woman, officials withdrew acceptance and she sued. The twenty-year-old was in and out of courts for two and a half years, fighting for admission. She reported to school twenty pounds overweight and left before the end of the first week.

One friend of mine blames Jane Fonda, Gloria Steinem and other fit feminists for not being at her house every day with Stairmasters and rice cakes. I wish Shannon Faulkner had been able to go the distance, but at least she opened the chink in the Citadel's legal armor. She did a lot, and going through still more years of abuse would probably be a lot to ask of one young person.

One of us will be along again soon. Whether it's Shannon

Faulkner or somebody twenty pounds lighter and twice as cute, the men of the Citadel are going to have to deal with us women sooner or later. We're in the boardrooms. We're in the human resources departments of the companies you want to work for. We're police officers and CEOs and anchorpersons and newspaper editors.

And we'll be waiting for you when you get out.

— *WVXU radio, September, 1995*

WHAT IF MISS AMERICA WORE A MUUMUU?

DID YOU WATCH the Miss America Pageant this year? In case you missed it, Leonard Horn would like you to know that he made every attempt to make the pageant "more relevant."

Mr. Horn is president of the event, now in its seventy-seventh year, and for the first time contestants were allowed to compete in either a two-piece or a one-piece bathing suit. This choice was left to each woman.

Now, lest these young women become giddy with this new freedom, the pageant officials were careful to specify standards. Regulations include "a full or modest rear" with the bottoms no more than an inch and a half below the navel. The women also were allowed to wear summer sandals.

"We want to encourage them to look their age," he says.

And, in fact, most women know that we are encouraged to look their age — that is, seventeen to twenty-four — for the rest of our natural lives. So, this is probably also relevant.

Mr. Horn told a reporter that he cringes at the contest being called a "beauty pageant." He says he prefers to call it a "scholarship program." There is, of course, only one relevant response to this. Hahahahahahahahahahahaha.

Some pageant officials have suggested that the bathing suit portion of the competition merely has to do with fitness and good health, ability to withstand a grueling public schedule. In that case, I guess that in addition to looking at his role in Democratic fund raising, we are really going to have to insist that we see Al Gore in a Speedo.

And what of the message this sends to the nation's youth? I don't mean young girls. They're already used to the idea that they need to starve themselves into acceptability when they're young. Later, they will be expected to carve away wrinkles and hoist their breasts.

But what about the young men of the country? Every year, they can see a fully sanctioned prime-time rating of women's bodies. Then we send them out into the workplace where they may be fired for noticing that Ms. Dilbert in the next cubicle has nice legs.

No wonder they're confused.

In the beginning, there was only bathing suits. No television. No talent competition. It was just eight young women in a bathing suit contest on the beach at Atlantic City. This was a gimmick concocted in September, nineteen twenty-

one, by the Avenue Hotelman's Association to keep tourists on the boardwalk after Labor Day.

An eighty-year-old man dressed as King Neptune came ashore from a yacht and led the women to Garden Pier. Later on, of course, the man became Bert Parks. The next year, fifty-eight women showed up to compete for the crown. Mary Catherine Campbell, Miss Ohio, won the second contest and set the tone for the future. Ohio is always a contender, and anybody who has three names stands a better chance of winning.

It wasn't until the nineteen forties that they added the scholarship money, and Lee Meriwether was the first Miss America crowned on television. I'm not sure when they started quizzing the finalists, giving them the opportunity to tell us their dearest wish is for world peace and the opportunity to star in a major motion picture.

But this year, for the first time, "without censorship or the involvement of the Miss America Organization," according to ABC, they were quizzed by a professional journalist. Nancy Glass of American Journal, formerly a reporter for PM Magazine, Sneak Previews and Inside Edition, was chosen to "ask the tough questions."

I guess Maureen Dowd and Susan Faludi were unavailable.

Anyway, the young contestants are talented. And they do have brains. Answering the "tough questions," they seem like nice people. But they still have to parade down a ramp, dressed in almost nothing.

The Miss America Pageant is a full-body beauty contest. And as long as young women have to take off their clothes to qualify as winners, it is silly to pretend it's anything better.

— *September, 1997*

BARBIE'S BOY TOY

KEN IS BARBIE'S boyfriend, and I am sorry to notice that she has not treated him kindly. He has stood by this doll for thirty-five years without ever being linked to another woman and with absolutely no commitment from her. Of course, how could she possibly commit to a relationship when she doesn't even know what she wants to be?

One year she's a veterinarian, and then she signs on as an airline pilot in roller skates. (I may be wrong about the roller skating part, but I definitely know she spent far too much time parading around our house in her underwear.)

Ken has been by her side during her astronaut phase and the glitter hair disaster, not to mention the Air Force and Dr. Barbie. Some of us remember Bubble Cut Barbie, Big Hair Barbie, Hippie Barbie and Jackie Kennedy Barbie, when she wore a pillbox but scorned the signature Jackie Kennedy square-toed, low-heeled shoes.

Barbie prefers slut shoes whether she's a physician or UNICEF ambassador. I think she has high arches and low morals.

Some women blame Barbie for everything from teen-age anorexia to breast implants. If our fixation on big breasts and lean bodies is from Brainwash Barbie, then I fear that a generation of America's children is going to grow up wanting to look like purple dinosaurs. Worse, they're going to be expecting Ken out there in the dating arena.

If young girls are getting their information about self-worth from Barbie and Ken, then the future men of America are in terrible trouble. Impressionable girls are going to grow up thinking they can just run around from wonderful career to wonderful career in their underwear and slut shoes and Ken will always be there to wax the Dream Car and vacuum the Dream House.

This guy has never strayed. Not only has he followed Barbie around like a dog for nearly four decades, but he never opens his mouth and is immediately available as an escort whenever she decides to have a Dream Date. You notice that there has never been a Golfing Ken or and ESPN Ken or a Remote Control Ken or a Male Pattern Baldness Ken.

Shaving Fun Ken's beard grows back five minutes after it's removed. I think you'll agree that this indicates a remarkable testosterone level, yet he is content to live in the shadow of this successful woman.

I don't think Ken and Barbie bear responsibility for the state of society. There never was a Dropout Barbie or a Crack-Head Ken. They're just dolls. And if we want our kids to have better role models, maybe we're just going to have to give them some real ones.

— *February, 1996*

Five

SEASON'S GREETINGS:
HO-HO-HO,
HABARAGANI AND BOO

"Tickle me."
—Elmo

No Halloween? That's
a Scary Thought

THIS IS PROBABLY politically and socially incorrect, but I'm going to notice publicly that we seem to have lost our perspective. Not to mention our sense of humor.

I am not speaking of the suspension from school of a six-year-old boy, accused of sexual harassment after he kissed a little girl on the cheek. I am not speaking of a nation united in debate over the crime of spitting on a baseball umpire. This is a country that puts up with rape, robbery and murder. But we draw the line at spitting on sports officials.

No, I am speaking of the flaw in America's character that compels it to ruin perfectly good holidays.

First of all, the very word holiday means "a day in which one is exempt from work." The only people who take this seriously are government employees. The rest of us are lucky to be able to sneak off an hour early for a green beer on St. Patrick's Day.

It's not bad enough that we have been denied the option of blowing our fingers off on the Fourth of July. Or that Abe Lincoln and George Washington don't get their own birthdays anymore. It's not bad enough that Christmas shopping begins in August. And that Easter baskets are now pre-packaged, including already-dyed hard-boiled eggs.

Now we are corrupting Halloween.

A pastor canceled a Halloween party at his church because he says it "promotes the occult."

Promotes the occult? Give me a break. Halloween promotes wearing costumes — cute when you're young, scary when you're older — preferably homemade. Next to science projects, most mothers' worst nightmare is the annual making of Halloween costumes.

Luckily, I come from a large family, so we recycled the costumes with customized personal touches. For instance, my Aunt Flora, an excellent seamstress, made a bee costume for my cousin, Hank. Wings, stinger, stripes, the works. The next year, my cousin Sara wore the bee suit with a crown. Her queen bee was a big hit, and one year later the suit fit my brother, Steven, who carried an ax and told everyone he was a killer bee.

When my turn came, the suit was a little the worse for wear. The killer bee had spilled grape Kool-Aid down the front of it. My mother, a resourceful woman, tied an apron over the purple stain and I marched in the parade as Aunt Bee.

Then, of course, there was beggar's night and the really, truly true meaning of Halloween. Candy. More candy. The kind of candy that ruins your dinner and rots your teeth. Enough bubble gum to send us to orthodontia hell.

This was all collected amid satisfying and totally untrue rumors that some fiend was handing out apples with razor blades inside. Our parents didn't worry because we were all begging in our own neighborhood, knocking on familiar doors.

This was before children were loaded into vans and driven into subdivisions where houses are closer together. In fact, people with long driveways usually gave the best stuff because they got fewer visitors. The best stuff was chocolate, but Tootsie Rolls, caramels, popcorn balls and candy cigarettes also were desirable. We did not appreciate apples or boxes of raisins, which we could get at home.

I feel sorry for kids today. Not only are they walking around in pre-packaged Power Ranger and Barney suits, but I have heard that certain households are passing out fast-food gift certificates and granola bars. From here, we are just one short, ugly step to orange rolls of dental floss and sandwich bags filled with brussels sprouts.

Myself, I pledge to distribute treats blacklisted by the American Dental Association. I will check the nutrition label and, if the item has any niacin or iron or vitamins, I will feed it to the dog. At my house, we will revive the ancient and honorable tradition of doing something that has absolutely no socially redeeming value. In the olden days, it was known as "fun."

— *November, 1996*

WISHING YOU A VERY EARLY CHRISTMAS

HAVE YOU NOTICED that the Christmas season begins earlier every year? I'll bet all the anal retentives had their shopping done by Labor Day. And they didn't have any trouble finding holiday paper and ribbon. And Christmas Muzak in the stores. Not that I'm one of those spoilsports who gripe about the commercialization of Christmas. Personally, I think getting material goods is a perfectly acceptable Christmas tradition, and it's probably our patriotic duty to boost the economic recovery by consuming as much as possible.

So I stand ready to receive as many gifts as anyone wants to give me, the more expensive and frivolous the better. I'm prepared to fax you a copy of my preferences because, although I think it's more blessed to give than to receive, I say it's more blessed to receive something you like. For my part, I'm going to spend until my Visa card explodes.

It's the least we can do for an industry that has been roughed up so ruthlessly over the past few years. When was the last time you paid full price for a suit? And while you have your wallet out, please try to spend as much money as possible in your downtown, your central business district. If you don't, I have it on good authority that they are going to hire an outside consultant, start another agency, hire some staff, then use your tax money to pay for it all. When they could be using this money to buy Christmas presents for me.

Retailers are mad as hell, and they're not going to take it anymore. Their message is clear. If we don't buy our brains out this year, they are going to start hanging the mistletoe even earlier next year. They're going to start sooner and sooner until we buy as much as they think we should.

So, my recommendation to you is to get your buns out there this year and shop. If you don't, I will consider it your fault when Santa turns up next August in a string bikini.

— National Public Radio,
September, 1995

THE DAY WHEN ONLY
TURKEYS ARE STRESSED

THANKFUL? I'LL TELL you why I'm thankful. I'm grateful we still have one unencumbered holiday left. Thanksgiving Day is when we gather simply to eat too much, watch too much football and wonder why cranberries are included in the celebration.

We don't have to shop or color eggs. We don't need special clothes. You will not receive a card with a form letter from your college roommate telling you her son's SAT scores. Except for the football marathon, things are pretty much like the Thanksgiving Day of my childhood. And yours, I'm guessing.

The cooks have changed. And maybe in some households, the turkey has become more exotic. I understand some of them baste themselves now. This is a shame. One of the best things about the day was when my grandmother opened the oven to baste the turkey and the aroma filled her house.

We were such a bunch — about three dozen — that no single turkey was big enough to feed us all. So my aunts brought venison and squirrel and rabbit, courtesy of my uncles who hunted. "Sit up straight. Use your napkin. Watch out for buckshot."

A lot of families, I hear, designate a children's table. Ours didn't. You ate with your mom and dad and brothers and sisters. No matter what your customary relationship with your siblings, it was understood that on this day, there would be no pinching, no bickering, no tattling.

Likewise, adults were allowed to argue about safe topics such as religion and politics, but Grandma wouldn't let them talk about more perilous subjects, such as hair. "Why don't you get a haircut, Jeff? You look like a girl." Forbidden.

The littlest kid got the highchair. The others sat on books if they needed them to reach their plates. Seating always included an old chair missing its back for as long as any of us could remember. Every year, a near ritual was when whoever had The Chair leaned back and both feet flew up, smacking the underside of the table. Everybody grabbed for the glasses. Some milk, some water. But most of us, even the kids, had wine.

My grandfather was Italian.

If Grandma was the heart of Thanksgiving, he was the soul, bellowing orders from his seat at the head table. "Put a little gravy on the dressing. Don't take that, David, unless you're going to eat the whole thing. Pass the squash."

He loved any excuse to cook and to eat. He handled beverages, side dishes and the cleanup. After bolting his food, he would turn his formidable energy to clearing. The slow eaters learned to eat with one hand and hold their plate with the other.

After dinner, the women and older girls were incarcerated in the kitchen with Grandpa. Soap suds flew everywhere, and your dish towel had to be wringing wet before he'd issue a new one. Silverware was counted. Inevitably, a spoon or fork was missing, and somebody had to paw through the garbage.

The older boys were in charge of folding up chairs and tables. The men were in charge of playing cards and drinking beer.

Off in a corner, my cousin Mickey was organizing the Thanksgiving play. She did this every year to avoid the possibility that she might have to dry some dishes or sift through turkey bones and bread crusts looking for a teaspoon.

To be fair, she did have a flair for drama. She wanted to be a lion tamer when she grew up. Mickey is a junior high school teacher, so I guess she got her wish. Anyway, she'd round up the little kids and dress them up as Pilgrims and

Indians. They'd re-create the first Thanksgiving, as they imagined it might have been.

"Sit up straight, John."

"Use your napkin, Priscilla."

"Watch out for buckshot, Squanto."

I love this holiday, a celebration of generosity. I will spend the day remembering Pilgrims and Indians and Grandpa and Grandma. I'll try to remember that the main idea was peace and sharing, not turkey or football. Maybe it's a lesson we could remember the day after. And the day after that. Maybe it's a lesson we could remember all year long, even without a turkey. Starting now.

No pinching. No bickering. No tattling.

— November, 1996

WISHING YOU A POLITICALLY INCORRECT DAY

THIS YEAR, I am going to muster the courage to just come right out and wish people a "Merry Christmas." And if that's not appropriate, I'm going to figure out what is and say that instead. I'm finished with the politically correct and colorless "Happy Holidays."

If you ask me, that's just a cheap way to say, "Maybe you have an important holiday around now, but I don't know for sure and I'm not interested in learning." It's the December equivalent of "Dear Occupant," and it further diminishes and commercializes a sacred season.

Surely, wishing a happy Christian day on an atheist or a Buddhist or a Jew isn't shoving an alien religion down their throats. When I wish somebody a Merry Christmas, I really just mean I wish all good things for them. I don't mean that I think they ought to abandon their customs and go to my church.

And surely, if you know somebody well enough to wish them a Merry Christmas, and they'd like for you to know a little more about them, they might say something like, "Thanks, I hope your Christmas is merry, too. I will be celebrating the first day of Ramadan."

Or simply, "And I wish you a Happy Kwanzaa."

Surely we can do that, can't we?

Thanksgiving is the official starting gun for the holiday season. It's worth remembering that this is more than just three weeks of shopping and glitter and ads for Chia pets. It's also worth noting that although the Pilgrims and Indians sat down together to share food, they did not dress up in each other's clothes and insist that their way was the only one.

The Jews have the right idea about this sort of thing. Of course, they've had a lot of time to think about it. More than two thousand years ago, the Jewish followers of Judas Maccabaeus began civilization's first recorded flight for personal liberty and religious freedom.

Hanukkah is the celebration of their victory and celebrates the right to religious freedom of all people. Jews light the menorah each day, exchange gifts and serve latkes.

The other big celebration at about the same time of year is not religious at all. Kwanzaa is a celebration of African culture. The greeting is "Habaragani?" That means, "What's the news?" in Swahili. Every day for seven days, the last week of the calendar year, celebrants light a candle representing unity, self-determination, collective work and responsibility, cooperative economics, purpose, creativity and faith.

"These seven principles are what we instill into our children," says an African-American friend, "because that's instilling it for our future and for everybody."

Well put.

So, Merry Christmas, Happy Hanukkah and Habaragani. Let's celebrate them all. And just tell me if you'd rather I wished you a happy Nirvana Day or Naw-Ruz. I want to know.

The holiday season is the time of year when we can all remind each other that we don't have to be exactly alike to share this planet in peace. That would be, I believe, a most politically correct holiday.

— *December, 1996*

THE ANNUAL SHOPPING FRENZY

WELL, HO, HO, HO. I don't have my Christmas shopping done yet. Do you? If you do, I don't think we can be friends, although I still adore my Aunt Patty, and she does her shopping months before Christmas. In fact, I would be very surprised if she doesn't have several items for the Christmas after next. She also changes her shelf paper every spring and cleans behind the refrigerator. You are either born this way or you're not.

I'm not.

This is why I have to fight my way into the stores every year, rubbing elbows with everybody else who's as irresponsible as I am. We are not a nice group of people when we are panicky. Just ask the Wal-Mart clerk who was mowed down by a group of rabid parents in search of Tickle Me Elmo. Or just watch our behavior in the parking lot of any mall, where shoppers are stalked for their parking spaces as soon as they leave the store.

While we are humiliating ourselves in search of Beanie Babies, Aunt Patty is probably sitting down with a big glass of egg nog and organizing her cookies by size and color. Or maybe she is dyeing Easter eggs. I am in the aisles of toy stores and specialty shops, and I can tell you I'd rather be at a Metallica concert.

It would be more civilized and quieter.

Do you know that they now have learning toys and computer games for newborns? Apparently, kids can come right down the chute and find out how to spell umbilical. Pathetic, computer-illiterate grandparents mill around the baffling array of "educational" toys, trying to snag a kid to ask for advice.

Barbie has her own lounge and marketing center in the middle of most toy stores, where you can buy ninety-seven million (by actual count) different dolls, each with her own outfit. Conspicuous Consumption Barbie also has her own talking makeup mirror, horse, answering machine and camera.

Greedy Barbie also owns several residences and vehicles, including a roadster, a minivan and a sport-utility vehicle. Meanwhile, Ken doesn't even have his own remote control for the TV in the Barbie Dream House. And he has put up with this situation for more than thirty-five years.

Perhaps he *is* anatomically correct.

You will not catch the Barbie toy company in the same boat with the Tickle Me Elmo toy company, which underestimated the passion for this little red monster in nineteen ninety-six. Mattel has produced enough Barbies to satisfy civilization to the end of the millennium.

My daughter, who is showing some shop-ahead tendencies she must have gotten from her father's gene pool, purchased Elmo several weeks before Elmo appeared on the Rosie O'Donnell Show, which apparently does for toys what Oprah does for books.

But the buying public is fickle. This year, Elmo might just end up on the markdown tables with the leftover Christmas ornaments and Disney Dalmatians, including a Wet 'n' Wizzer plush pup that defeats the purpose of getting a fake dog in the first place, if you ask me.

Look for plenty of surplus devices you can heat in your microwave then apply to body parts, such as backs or aching shoulders. They also sell microwaveable seats and socks. They should sell separate microwave ovens for those of us who would rather not have our food come out of something that also cooks things people sit on or put on their feet.

I have never been depraved enough to actually shop on Christmas Eve, but I have pushed it close to the wire. By the time I get my Yuletide act together, ordering by mail is out of the question, as is anything engraved or monogrammed.

What finally happens is that on the eve of Christmas Eve, I am lured by the very items I sneered at when I have more time. Microwaveable knee pads. Chia Pets. Weed Whackers. Thighmasters.

So, anyway, I'm proud to say that, thanks to me, when Aunt Patty is alphabetizing her soup cans next spring, she can turn on the pantry light with her very own Smart Clapper.

— *December, 1996*

Six

YOUR TAX DOLLARS AND OTHER TOXIC WASTE

*"That stuff about the
Bengals wasn't as dumb
as your usual dumb stuff."*
— Marty, semi-anonymous
media critic

WASHINGTON AND THE
DOO-DOO THING

I'M SORRY TO rain on the most recent inaugural parade, because it is wonderful, really, to renew our government every four years. Without a revolution. But I believe that we all have noticed how much money was squandered on this year's extravaganza.

More than a million dollars was spent for each of the thirty-five words in the oath of office. It cost forty-four million dollars, including thirteen million dollars which belonged to taxpayers. I would rather have had the money.

Dozens of bands marched. A limousine was dispatched to pick up the First Comedienne, Whoopie Goldberg. Entertainers included Aretha Franklin, Stevie Wonder, Kenny Rogers, Yo-Yo Ma, Candice Bergen and Michael Douglas.

Ticket holders included men in dinner jackets and women in mink coats. The women in minks were asked to hide their coats under their chairs when the television cameras arrived. There were no less than eight inaugural balls. There were tumblers, a polka band, a mariachi band and horse troops from across America. A horse-drawn pioneer wagon re-enacted the Mormons' arrival in Salt Lake City. There were equestrian teams from Culver Military Academy in Indiana. In all, three hundred forty-eight horses walked up Pennsylvania Avenue.

This brings me to the terrible waste.

Forty-five schoolchildren wearing clown outfits and carrying shovels were asked to scoop up horse droppings along the parade route. I don't mind Whoopie's limo. And who could object to a polka band?

I just think it's silly and wasteful to buy clown outfits for a group of innocent school children on poop patrol. Especially when there were scores of perfectly good congressmen just sitting around in the bleachers.

— *WVXU radio, January, 1997*

TIME FOR MIKE TO COME OUT OF THE SHADOWS

PART OF THE reason a lot of people are ticked off about the new Bob Bedinghaus Memorial Taxatorium and Athletic Complex is because they just don't like Mike Brown. And they don't much like the idea of setting him up in multi-million-dollar splendor, even if it's only a half-cent, even if it's good for the whole city in the long run.

Marge is bad enough, but at least we like her. Yes, we do. It's our dirty little secret, America. Although she has used the N-word more times than F. Lee Bailey, although she flirted with the over-the-river boys, although her polyester is shinier, her cannons are looser and her purse strings are tighter than almost anybody else we can think of, there are people who will defend her to the death.

Not because we're closet racists or because we felt a thrill of local pride when she discussed Schottzie's nipples with David Letterman, but because we know her.

Nobody knows Mike.

Marge blabs and blabs and blabs to anybody who will listen. She pouts and threatens, but we know it's all bluff. She loves it here.

Mike issues terse little bulletins with locked jaw. He does not bluff.

She is Margie Unnewehr from Diehl Road on the West Side. He is Harvard by way of Cleveland. She lets her dogs lick her on the lips. His lips don't move when he talks.

She hung around the family lumber business, and her daddy called her Butch. He hung around the sidelines of the Browns, and his daddy called him legal counselor and negotiator.

We hyphenated, enlightened, liberated women hate it when Marge sings the "I'm just a widow woman trying to make it in a man's world" blues. Furthermore, we know that she thinks we should be home having babies, and she calls us gals.

But we love the idea that when Charlie Schott died, she didn't just hand over his brick plants and car dealerships to some male trust officer. She fired all the guys who tried to collect expense money for attending her husband's funeral, then she got the unions to work with her and stuck it to the Detroit wheels who didn't think a woman should own a car dealership.

When she was invited to a black-tie affair closed to unescorted ladies, she showed up with a dancing bear.

Maybe her Indian Hill neighbors don't like her. She's probably a little high-profile. She did the charity gig when Charlie was alive, but she was never a "museum lady." Some sports writers hate her in a curiously bitter way. I can't imagine one of them calling Happy Chandler a "silly old man."

But regular people like her.

Mike Brown's Indian Hill neighbors probably think he's okay. He has cats, not a big bunch of noisy dogs. He doesn't have parties where you buy tickets and have your car parked by a valet. The trouble is, the folks in Indian Hill and at the tables at the Queen City Club won't be paying all the freight for Mike's stadium. A big chunk will come from the rest of us, the ones who won't be buying the fancy stadium boxes or who would rather go to a soccer game or have the money spent on our kids' schools.

So, I have a modest suggestion for you, Mr. Brown. Charm us. You can do it. Be a photo op every once in a while. You don't have to get a dog or anything. But why don't you give a painting to the art museum or a tiger to the zoo? Chair some big thing like United Way or even just serve on a few volunteer boards. You know, sort of help out.

If John Pepper can run Procter and still mentor a high school kid, you should be able to walk for the March of Dimes.

Let us get to know you.

The business community wants your Bengals, and all of

us in the cheap seats knew from the beginning that they'd hold their breath until their chips turned blue if we didn't cough up. It was inevitable that you'd get your stadium. You don't even have to win any games, although that'd be nice.

You pride yourself on being a private man, but this is public money. So since we are going to pay for everything anyway, just let us like you a little.

— *July, 1995*

DO WE WANT THE BENGALS AT ANY COST?

DO WE HAVE buyer's remorse? Well, I think maybe we do. After an enormously persuasive sales pitch, the voters of Hamilton County agreed to a sales tax to build stadiums for the Bengals and the Reds. We were promised an easy payment plan and a few extra frills in exchange for our business. You know, frills like property-tax rebates and money to repair our schools.

If we had the option of choosing just the Reds, it was in print so fine that we didn't see it. We bought the deluxe package. Loaded, as they say. We even sprang for a practice field for the football team. On the river.

A little time has passed.

We are like a family that agreed to buy a great big camper and a smaller family sedan. We can make the payments. But maintenance on the camper has turned out to be more expensive than we were led to believe it would.

In fact, it's so big that we may have to park the sedan on the street. Or wedge it into the garage.

The salesman isn't as nice as he was when he was making the sale. And it occurs to us that we don't really use the camper that much — maybe eight or ten times a year. It's not very versatile. You can't exactly use it to make a run to the grocery store. In fact, you can't use it for anything else.

We use the sedan a lot. It's more dependable than the camper, and, actually, the neighbors seem to be more impressed with it than the great big gas hog. Truth to tell, everybody in the family seems to like the sedan better. It's more fun.

Besides, we can't help noticing all the other things we could do with the money we are going to spend on this expensive toy. And how easy it would be to park the sedan if we didn't have to work around the other vehicle.

And now it turns out that the camper salesman doesn't like our original deal. He's threatening to back out. To sell his vehicle to somebody else. This might be our chance to let him.

This was not a decision we reached easily. Remember Tim Mara and his "Taxed Enough Already?" And Mike Brown, a private and solemn man, actually became a public spokesman and photo op. And we bought what he was selling.

A great big camper that maybe we don't need after all.

— *March, 1997*

UNIVERSAL LEGAL COVERAGE

TORT REFORM HAS such a nasty ring. It makes it sound as though attorneys have been doing something slightly unsavory, such as making it impossible to turn around without getting sued for your back teeth. Besides, this is small potatoes, reform-wise. I think it's time to begin the debate on universal legal coverage.

Instead of our government arranging for all of us to get affordable, mediocre medical care from physicians who would become, more or less, government employees, they could arrange for every American to have an attorney anytime we need one. And the attorneys would just get paid what the government thinks is fair. And they would have to justify any suing they do and their number of billable hours would be regulated by people who don't know the difference between an amicus brief and a Fruit of the Loom brief.

If they devote too many hours to, say, a simple damage claim, they would just get paid for the average number of hours the government thinks it's worth.

I think this is a great idea, and I can't wait for Hillary to get to work on it. In fact, I think we're in the middle of a legal-care crisis right now. The nation's law schools keep churning out attorneys, who are pretty much unregulated, except by each other. The more lawyers out there trying to make a living, the more lawsuits there are. And you can see what has happened.

The insurance companies are demanding reform. Because the last thing the insurance companies want to do is to spend your premium money on you.

I'm not kidding. I think I'm on to something. I was really sick once and I was really sued once, and I can tell you that getting sued was a lot worse. The prognosis was more uncertain. It was more expensive. And a lot scarier.

— National Public Radio,
April, 1994

A SALES PITCH THAT GETS YOU COMING AND GOING

JUST IN CASE you always thought North Carolina was "First in Flight," Ohio wants you to know that it is the "Birthplace of Aviation." Both states are using these slogans on their license plates, which are supposed to act as dinky little billboards to lure tourists.

Frankly, I can't believe either slogan will be a big draw. I'd vote for something more along the lines of "Giving Away Free Popcorn" or "Mime-Free Zone" or "The Fat-Free State." But Ohio and North Carolina think the Wrights are where it's at.

State Rep. Marilyn Reid, who led the fight to amend Ohio's plates, says the Wrights were only in North Carolina because it's windy there and they'd rather crash into sand and water than trees and pasture. She says the new plates will attract more visitors to the Wrights' home in Dayton. I don't get it.

We Ohioans already know that the Wrights were born here. And we're not going to travel here because we're already here. We should try to get our slogan on some other state's license plate. Maybe we could exchange with, say, Minnesota, which could brag about being "Home of the Spam Cookoff" on Ohio's plates. Or we could just use my bumper.

Every motorist in Ohio who thinks that "Birthplace of Flight" is a dopey way to attract visitors could just pay an extra dollar for a license plate that has a crisp six-digit number. Blue on a white background. No cardinal. No slogan.

I would be willing to accept this money to put a more complete message across the entire bumper of my car. Then I would drive to places where people hang around just before they decide to spend thousands of dollars in search of attractions such as the World's Largest Ball of Twine or Spam festivals or famous aviation sites.

How about: "Bring your family to the place where the Wright brothers were born and would have stayed except they heard there was a high wind in North Carolina. So, if you're looking for fun, and you do not particularly need wind, sand or an ocean, then come to Ohio."

I think this should fly, don't you?

— *WVXU, January, 1997*

Do We Really Need
To Feel The Pain?

NOW MIGHT BE a good time to think about tax reform. We all know that we spend a great big chunk or our lives working for the government and that the average American family pays more in taxes than it spends on food, clothing and shelter combined. And that we'll be working until the middle of July to pay next year's tax bill.

We know this.

But most of the year, we are in deep denial. Until April fifteenth. Then we think about it quite a bit. We suspect that we are paying for things that we'll never use and that everybody else is getting more for their tax dollar than we are.

We know for sure that somehow we've missed a legitimate deduction, thereby sending too much of our hard-earned cash to Washington to be squandered (legitimate deductions for other people are known as "loopholes").

We worry that we may have innocently done one of those red-flag things that will make someone in the IRS Asylum go "Tee hee hee. Let's audit this loser."

The tax code, for those of you out there too busy pawing through your shoe box full of receipts to count, is spelled out in five hundred fifty-five million words, not including eight thousand pages of appendixes and fine print. It is monstrous and incomprehensible. About two-thirds of us pay somebody else to sort through it for us (Our tax consultant is "aggressive." Other people's are "shysters.")

House Majority Leader Dick Armey started talking about the flat tax in nineteen ninety-four, and it seemed like a good idea then. Of course, like most good ideas in Washington, this one has been attacked and talked to death and watered down and massaged and porked up. But it's still alive, and I will leave the final mugging to those who do it best.

Instead, I'd like to discuss Dick Armey's bad idea, which everybody has ignored. Bad ideas are the ones that sneak aboard unrelated bills, and the next thing you know you are stuck with them for eternity — or until Robert Byrd retires. Whichever comes first.

Mr. Armey has said that he thinks it would be a good idea to collect our income taxes every month, doing away with payroll deductions. In other words, we'd get all our money, then put it aside and pay the government at the end of the month.

Dick? Hello? Can you say "deadbeat?" Can you say "collection agency?" Can you say "another big bureaucracy?"

Paying our own taxes every month, according to Mr. Armey, would help us taxpayers "focus on how our money is being spent and how much." If the government really wants to rub our noses in it, they could keep the money and just send us monthly reports.

How about:

"Dear taxpayer, thank you for the one thousand, three hundred thirty-three dollars and thirty-three cents you gave us this month. We used it to buy a new toilet seat for Air Force One. We're certain Stan Chesley felt a little thrill of local pride during the President's last trip to Cincinnati."

Or, "Thanks a lot for the two thousand, one hundred seventy-three dollars we got from you this month. We sent it directly to Howard Metzenbaum's government pension fund. Someday, you may be able to tell your friends that you helped buy a trout farm."

Or, "Your government is grateful for the one thousand, five hundred dollars this month. You now own a pothole in Montana and a conceptual artist in Tennessee."

Or, "We appreciate your nine hundred seventy-three dollars and forty-two cents. We have ordered a new VCR and the Buns of Steel tape for the Congressional gym. We had a couple of bucks left, so we're buying a new feather boa for Big Bird.

Myself, I sort of like not being beaten over the head with how they're going to be using the money I've just signed over. But then, I always ask my dentist for plenty of novocain. I know they're going to pull my tooth, but I don't need to experience the pain to believe it's gone.

— *April, 1996*

NEW CHANCE TO CREATE DOGGY DEBT

IT APPEARS THAT our deadbeat dog finally may have the chance to pay us back. While Schottzie Two has been out selling Buicks and Frazier's Eddie has been raking in the product-endorsement bucks, Misty Pulfer has been doing exactly nothing to improve the family fortunes.

But her days as a non-productive, Iams-guzzling hair-ball factory and flea ranch may be over. She is going to get her own Visa card. Believe me, it's none too soon. Misty, a beautiful and dignified collie, came to live with us about a year ago. She was four years old and free. What a laugh. If you have ever had a pet, you know the purchase price is merely an initiation fee.

After that, there's the gynecologist, the dermatologist, the doggie vacation motel, flea spray, heartworm pills, pedicures, the hairdresser, groceries. I expect that she's going to need bifocals and her own phone line any day now.

We're not complaining, but we do worry that Misty has no real appreciation for the value of a dollar. We have spoiled her.

She came to us a rather accomplished adult dog. Oh, don't get me wrong, she never told us that Timmy was in the well or that Gramps was trapped in a barn fire, but when we said "sit," she sat. She trotted obediently to heel on our left and she never jumped up on us and she only ate dry dog food and she liked to sleep outside. Or at least she did so without complaining.

Misty also was completely housebroken. This means that she would do her business outside if we guessed that she needed to. And got her there right away, as soon as the mood was upon her. Otherwise, she could not be responsible for what would happen. As you can imagine, we have become slaves to her moods. And alert, very alert.

She has made remarkable progress under our care and instruction. When we say "sit," she growls at the cat. She is now, if I may brag a little, much more versatile on the leash and walks on both our left and our right sides and sometimes she pulls us and sometimes we pull her. At the command "down," she looks puzzled, then hurt, then leaves the room.

If we speak sharply to her, she drools uncontrollably.

She loves to jump on us in greeting, particularly if she is muddy and we are dressed to go someplace. Although her lineage is long and distinguished, she is not too proud to drink from the porcelain punch bowl. Dry dog food depresses her, and at night she likes to sleep at the foot of our bed.

My husband thinks that in another month we'll have her biting people.

Maybe the folks at Visa who sent her the letter can teach her a little self-control and discipline, although I have my doubts. When I review our recent history together, I am plagued by a terrifying image — me up to my knees in dog biscuits and rawhide bones — with Misty under the bed, hiding from the bill collector.

This credit card, according to the brochure, offers Misty one-hundred-thousand-dollar automatic travel accident insurance. I don't know if this is standard or if somebody at Visa got a whiff of the backseat of our car. I've never priced one of those little hanging fir trees, but surely they can't be that steep.

Misty also can take advantage of a credit line of up to five thousand dollars. Perhaps this freeloader will remember those of us who have been so generous with her. Maybe I will come home from work some day to find a big-screen TV and a bread machine. What do I care if she maxes out? It's the bank's fault for making it too easy for just any old dog to get credit. She can declare bankruptcy. Or get a job.

She could be the first dog in America to admit that she has a spending disorder. We could be on The Jerry Springer Show: "Collies Who Spend Too Much and the Women Who Love Them."

Hey, wait a minute. My name appears on the card, too. It says they will emboss my dog's name right on the face of my new Visa card. You mean this is just another opportunity for me to be up to my humanoid ears in interest fees? I'm responsible for the dog's debts?

No thank you. She still owes me for the sweat shirt with Lassie's picture on it and the John Tesh CDs.

— *March, 1996*

Seven

THE DAYS OF WHINE
AND NOSES

*"When these kids are stuck
at home and the television set
quits working, you have a
disaster on your hands."*
—Ivan Steinberg

SNOWSTORMS BRING OUT
FLAKY SHOPPERS

JUST WHEN YOU thought you'd shoveled your way out, the weather hysterics are saying more snow is on the way. So, for heaven's sake, get out there and shop while you can.

During the last blizzard, in nineteen seventy-eight, we lived in Maineville, Ohio, at the end of a scenic quarter-mile lane. I would rather eat barbed wire than repeat that scenic experience. When the snow hit, we had plenty of the stuff you actually need: milk, canned food, meat, toilet paper.

We had none of the stuff you actually want.

After three days of a balanced diet, we were starting to get surly.

Our lane and the county's roads were impassable, but we had a couple of horses and we'd seen that Budweiser commercial of the Clydesdales sweeping majestically through the snow. So we saddled them up and headed for the grocery store down the road.

We limited ourselves to the essentials.

That is why, after fighting gale-force winds, sub-zero temperatures, three-foot-high drifts and two horses that had not seen the Budweiser commercial, we came back to the house with a carton of Parliament cigarettes, a bottle of Lambrusco wine, a bag of nacho cheese Doritos and a package of Fruit Stripe gum.

We suffered this latest monster snow in deepest, darkest Hyde Park.

But if you looked around the neighborhood, you would have thought we were all about to be stranded at the end of a quarter-mile lane for a month. Naturally, everybody was buying snow shovels and salt and fireplace logs. Ivan Steinberg of the Steinberg's electronics and appliance chain said shoppers also rushed out to buy TVs.

"When these kids are stuck at home and the television set quits working, you have a disaster on your hands."

Geez, that would be awful. The parents might have to talk to the kids or something.

What I really want to know is why everybody was lining up at the checkout counter at the grocery. Did they really think they were going to starve? Were they stocking up on pizza and beer? Were they afraid they'd be stuck at home with lots of kids and a serious Twinkie shortage?

Just before the White Death struck, I was too busy dodging shoppers wearing gum boots and crabby expressions to really audit their groceries. Now that the first snow has settled, I checked with local grocers to see what was on the menu for the feeding frenzy.

Sunshine Fine Foods in Hyde Park was wiped out of bread, milk and ground chuck. One woman braved the elements to dash inside for a pint of kraut. It was, I suppose, her version of Doritos.

Mary Bracke of Bracke Meats & Produce in Mt. Lookout Square says her customers hit the bread and milk hard, but they also cleaned the shelves of egg nog and "a lot of wine." This is more like it.

Barbara Murray, whose family owns Humberts' Meats in Westwood, says that when the delivery truck pulled up, "people were taking things out of the cartons before we could get them to the case." They sold record numbers of milk, potato chips, soup and lunchmeat. And bread. Really lots of bread. What are people doing with all this bread? Using it as insulation? Feeding the birds? Are they trading it for other more valuable things, such as Dove Bars?

At Keller's IGA in Clifton, Carl Clower says his customers hit the wine, beer and candles. "Actually," he says, "they bought a lot of everything. And we ran out of..."

Don't tell me, Carl. I think I know.

Bread.

"Right."

So after an exhaustive investigation into crisis management in Cincinnati, I think a pattern is clear. When the going gets tough, the tough buy bread.

— *January, 1996*

MEMO TO MS. NATURE:
WE SURRENDER

WE HAVE REALLY done it this time. She's thoroughly honked off, and we are paying the price. I'm speaking, of course, about Mother Nature, who appears to be bitterly angry. This seems more than just a bad mood, something bigger.

I think we're being punished.

Admittedly, I know less than nothing about global warming and cooling trends and barometric pressure and the ozone layer and Dopplers and storm systems and the greenhouse effect. That is why God created men in bad sport coats with pointers and weather maps.

The only thing I know for sure is that I surrender. I give up. Unconditionally. Unilaterally. Without honor. Especially without honor.

Does Mother Nature want us to save the Rain Forest? Does she think I'm using too much hair spray? Should I be driving a smaller car? Using less gasoline? Taking the bus? Carpooling? Should I be giving more money to the Save the Snow Leopard Fund? Is there a whale out there I should be saving?

Should I chain myself to the bulldozer next time a developer starts taking out trees? How about snail darters? Do you suppose she's happy with the way that turned out? Maybe I should nag my neighbors about recycling. Or pesticides.

Whatever it is, I'll do it.

Because I'm sick of fighting.

Last winter was bad enough. Cold. Snow. More cold. More snow. Schools were canceled, meetings postponed. The power went out. Pipes froze. Roofs leaked. Some of them collapsed. I-75 was like a bumper car caravan. Potholes on Columbia Parkway sent hubcaps flying to Westwood. But at least we could look forward to spring. Tornadoes and record-high winds.

Now it's rain. More rain. Roofs are leaking. Basements are flooded. It was the soggiest April on record, followed by a May that has set everybody's teeth on edge. We've gotten more than six inches of rain, and we're only a little more than halfway through the month.

I'm not positive, but I think I'm growing moss on my southside. I know that my front yard is a bog and the back yard is probably going to be a mosquito motel.

This is not funny anymore. Sewers are clogged. Mud slides have closed streets and roads. Race horses were evacuated from the track. The Boy Scouts had to postpone their jamboree. Riverboat restaurants were turning away customers who couldn't get up the gangplank.

When our food, our gambling and our Boy Scouts are at risk, it seems clear that something must be done. How can we make it up to you, Mother Nature? Or would you prefer Ms. Nature? Your weathership? Queen of the Clouds? Princess of Precipitation? Ruler of the Rain? Chancellor of the low-pressure system? How can we make amends? Whatever it is, we'll do it.

Otherwise, I think we all know what we can expect. Heat. More heat. Record heat. Heat with humidity. Sticky. One continuous bad hair day. Wet socks. Mildew. Great big bills for air conditioning. Cranky babies. Cranky adults.

Let's do it. Let's make peace. We have nothing to lose but our planet.

— March, 1996

LITTLE TOWN, BIG TROUBLE

THE TOWN, AS far as you can see, is under dirty, brown water. McDonald's golden arches are just half moons. There's an IGA sign but no grocery, A Shell sign but no station.

Not to mention the houses.

Falmouth, Kentucky, was hit hard.

Susan Field shivers under a dingy orange blanket, huddled in the lobby of Pendleton County High School. She and her three boys have been here since about two a.m. After a night on hard red plastic chairs, they ate cheese crackers from a vending machine for breakfast.

Brad Field, twelve, has put his watch and Swiss army knife on a window sill to dry. Everything else was left behind when the pickup truck with volunteers from the fire department swooped in and told them to get in "right now."

It happened so fast.

Anita England left home with her three dogs and as many blankets as she could grab. Her car hit a wall of water and stalled. "the next thing I know I'm grabbing dogs and climbing into a truck," she says, shaking a soggy shoe.

Cars drive through the school parking lot, searching, "looking for kin." Families have been separated. Phones are out. The victims are scattered. The Red Cross has set up a shelter at a church. Several people were taken to the Falmouth Middle School, now surrounded by water.

Angela Gillispie keeps asking if anybody has heard anything about her fiance. "I haven't seen him since two a.m. He gave me his wallet and started swimming. His mom has rheumatoid arthritis and he was afraid they wouldn't get to her."

In the school gymnasium, four kids shoot hoops as patients from River Valley Nursing Home in Butler are carried in. The elderly people are taken to the school library, where a desk is moved aside for a portable oxygen tank. Nurses and volunteers stack their purses on a table. No one stands guard. No one needs to.

Outside, Army reservists in camouflage load blankets, food and water onto a flatbed truck carrying a boat. The supplies were brought in by area hospitals. A chopper arrived earlier with a doctor and a nurse. No one is in charge. And, apparently, no one needs to be.

Everyone finds something to do. Extension cords, chocolate pies, fried chicken, willing hands appear like magic. Down by the river, a yellow police tape stops traffic right at Godman's

Garage, just before the bridge over the south fork of the Licking River. The rain has stopped, but the river continues to rise.

Why, I wonder, do we worry every winter about a few snowflakes? Rain is more dangerous here, always has been. Last weekend, puddles became roiling ponds. Lakes dotted open fields and subdivisions. Falmouth was nearly washed away.

Nature at its worst.

People at their best.

— *March, 1997*

HEAT ALERT, WEATHER TRIVIA ON THE HORIZON

OKAY. IT'S SUMMERTIME. We're in Cincinnati. It's hot. It's humid. It gets this way every year. If you don't like it, why don't you move to Columbus? Then you can be hot and bored at the same time.

Excuse me, I'm a little cranky. I think it might be the heat.

I don't remember that it was ever this hot when I was a kid, but the almanac says it was one hundred degrees in August of nineteen fifty-four. I remember that year, but I don't remember any national emergencies. I don't remember a heat alert. Most of all, I don't remember sitting around complaining about the heat in the comfort of air conditioning.

In fact, air conditioning was so rare that movie theaters advertised it to give you another reason to come inside, just in case Milk Duds, Tab Hunter, the balcony, Sandra Dee, real popcorn and Elizabeth Taylor were not reason enough.

We had screens on our windows, and we used fans. When it was really blistering, sometimes we used auxiliary fans, those paper ones that you could get with the name of a funeral home on the back. We also went barefoot and ran though the yard sprinkler.

Do you suppose it feels so much hotter because somebody invented meteorologists, who in turn invented the heat index? That, of course, is a formula combining the temperature and the humidity to come up with a number that will make you really miserable. It's like the wind-chill factor, only in reverse.

Or maybe it got so hot because we got to be adults and have to face the sun in coats and ties and pantyhose.

If you think that you don't like those heat "emergencies," I can tell you that newspaper reporters really hate them. For one thing, they have to write weather stories. And there's really nothing to say. But they have to say it anyway.

You've always got your basic asphalt story, your kids-at-the-swimming-pool photo opportunity, your basic health department advisory. I think I overheard one reporter offer to buy another one a frozen yogurt and give her a thousand dollars if she'd take over the weather story assignment.

As far as the basic health department advice, in case you missed it, the official word is that we should decrease our physical activity and stay in the shade. We are also advised to drink plenty of water and wear loose, lightweight cotton clothing. Luckily, that was not advice we needed back in the nineteen fifties, as polyester had not reared its ugly head on the fashion horizon.

We probably also didn't need to be told to drink plenty of water, because that is mostly what was available when you were thirsty. We did not have nineteen varieties of Sunny Delight and two hundred fifty- seven kinds of cola. We drank Kool-Aid and lemonade. On really hot days, we even sold them.

Hey, wait a minute. I think this qualifies as a weather story.

I'll take double dutch chocolate yogurt and small, unmarked bills.

— *August, 1995*

COLD? GO WEST, YOUNG PERSON

THERE ARE MANY wonderful things about winter.

January is not one of them.

This is the month when everybody seems to be sneezing

or whining. I, myself, being extremely versatile, am doing both. Last year was bad enough. Cold. Snow. More cold. More snow. Schools were canceled, meetings postponed. The power went out. Pipes froze. Roofs collapsed. But this year has been almost worse. Dishonest. A tease.

It's really warm. No, it's really cold. It's going to snow. No, that will be freezing rain. Or just rain. Or just freezing.

If you want my advice (and there is no reason why you would), I'd say we'd all feel better if we took a trip. Instead of sniveling about the weather or our sinuses, let's just get out of town.

No amount of wishing is going to change the natural course of events. It's January. It's cold. It's wet one day, icy the next. And just to keep it interesting, this is the season when everybody is sick. Germs are spread, as most of us know, by children and management.

Children cannot help themselves. They are just little breeding centers for colds and flu, walking petri dishes. Anybody who has a child is sick most of the winter because we eat things that they discard. Also, we cannot help hugging and kissing them, even if their noses are runny. Then our noses are runny.

Those of us who are not infected by children are infected by our bosses. These people (and I think you know who you are) come crawling in to work, sick as dogs. They are scared to death that if they stay at home with their germs that the rest of us will get the idea that we can do the same thing.

All day long, they hide in their offices, probably with their feet up watching *The Young and the Restless* and drinking orange juice. They come out only occasionally so that we can see them — troupers on the job despite ill health. And the clear implication is that they are setting the example for the rest of us. Every once in a while, they stick their heads into your cubicle to sneeze. Pretty soon, everybody is sick. By then, management is at a conference in Aruba.

So, as I say, I would recommend a trip. But unless you have a company with an extremely liberal vacation policy, you will have to come back here while it's still cold. So my advice is to go someplace worse. May I suggest Billings, Montana?

There you will find subzero temperatures and about seven inches of snow. You can entertain the natives with tales of a city that panics and hurls salt all over itself at the prospect of what they might regard as mild precipitation.

Yes, Billings would be perfect. You should have no trouble finding a good parking space. Even people in Billings are leaving Billings. A woman from the Chamber of Commerce there told me that everybody she knows is getting out of town to go skiing in Bozeman or Red Lodge.

After a trip out West, when you get back here, you'll be grateful for a city that regards two inches of snow as a dangerous blizzard, and two and a half as white death. You will rediscover the charm of a city that rallies at the news of impending winter precipitation by running out and buying up all the available bread.

It would be a serious mistake to squander your precious vacation time on, say, Naples, Florida which is loaded with midwesterners. Temperatures there right now are in the high sixties and low seventies. So, if you go there, you'll start feeling right at home. Then, the next thing you know, it will be time to come back to the real Midwest, and it will be just as cold as it was when you left.

But it will feel worse.

So, if I were you I would get through this January in the time-honored tradition of worrying about snow that never materializes and buying up bread when it does. Or I would travel to Billings. If management says you can't have the time off, tell your boss you are packing a can of Lysol, and you're not afraid to use it.

— *January, 1997*

Eight

TRAVELS TO UNFAMILIAR PLACES, SUCH AS OUTER SPACE

*"If we can't trust you, we
won't tell you some of the
really bizarre things we know."*
—Woman at UFO support
group meeting

WINNING A SEAT WITH THE LOWER PRESS

PLEASE BELIEVE THAT I am not totally stupid. When I found out that I had a seat on the Presidential train to Chicago, I did not really think that Mr. Clinton and I would be sitting side by side in matching engineer hats, fighting over who gets to blow the whistle.

I knew that there might be others along on this trip. As it turns out, this is a very long train, one that you would not want to cross your personal intersection if you are in a hurry. And you don't exactly get to drop in at the last minute.

First, you have to fill out many, many pages of information, including, I noticed indignantly, your weight. I guess they want to put all us fat journalists in the seats with good springs. Or perhaps they are worried about special dietary requirements, such as whether we're likely to demand Cheetos and beer.

"All information on the White House Press sign-up sheet becomes BINDING." (Their caps, not mine. I think it's a cheap literary device. I use *italics* for emphasis.) So, although I would like to look more svelte just in case I get anywhere near George Stephanopoulos, I am BOUND (*bound*) not to lose a pound.

So be it. I had French fries for lunch.

The completed sign-up sheet was to be faxed to the White House Lower Press Office. The office, I hope, refers to its location and does not reflect any sort of caste system. You know, like I would be among the Lower Press, but Cokie Roberts would return her credentials to the Upper Brow Press Office and Don Imus would send his off to the Under-A-Rock Press Office.

As taxpayers, you will be pleased to learn that everything for the press corps is cash on the barrelhead. It cost *The Enquirer* three hundred dollars for me to ride from Columbus to Toledo. I believe I could have hired a limo with a bar and a TV for that, but then I'm a careful shopper. Modems, hotels, cellular phones and fax hookups are *a la carte*.

Demands were issued for credit-card numbers, along with ominous warnings about "reconciled charges," clearly just a way to make sure that the Clinton-Gore Ninety-Six Primary Committee does not get stuck with bills for macadamia nuts and Chivas from the hotel honor bar. A baffling blizzard of confirmations and further instructions included a note that some of us may be tapped to join the "jogging pool." Yipe, I'd rather be in the Big Mac pool or the doughnut-eating pool. Or the White House hot tub.

My plan has always been simply to meet the Leader of the Free World and get a train ride. I will be reporting from a cornfield in northern Ohio. I expect to be able to pass along important political information, such as whether James Carville really short-sheeted Sam Donaldson's bed. And I will investigate rumors that Al Gore has joined the Hair Club.

After all, I am traveling with the Lower Press.

— *August, 1996*

GOUGING BEGINS AT HOME

AS YOU KNOW, it's impolite to notice anything negative about Delta Air Lines. One of the big selling points used by the Chamber of Commerce when it's flogging the city to out-of-town businesses who might have heard unkind rumors about downtown decline is that Cincinnati is a Delta hub with international connections.

The Convention and Visitors Bureau may not be able to explain away the human-rights ordinance, but they can honestly promise that conventioneers can get in and out of Cincinnati easier than almost any other city in the country.

This is all very wonderful unless you are planning to travel with your own, personal money. Let's say you had decided not to go to an old boyfriend's wedding. Then word reaches you that because of the stress of wedding preparations, the bride-to-be has put on twenty-five pounds. You, on the other hand, have been aerobicizing your buns off. Literally.

Clearly you must make the trip.

You have not planned in advance. (Who knew? You had heard she was a former lingerie model who now owns her own computer software company. It was an honest mistake.) You will travel any time, day or night, but you want to fly out of Cincinnati. And return here. I hope money is no object.

Travelers out of Cincinnati pay on average eighty dollars more for a one-way ticket than residents in other U.S. cities, according to a federal study. Same peanuts. Same seats. Same oxygen masks. Same fat guy in the seat next to you hogging the armrest.

Just about everybody knows by now that if you drive to Dayton or Columbus or Indianapolis you can get a cheaper ticket than if you leave from here. Sometimes on the same Delta flight. The company has just announced cheap flights to Florida. But not from Cincinnati, of course.

And if we don't like it, that's tough. They're big. We need them, and they don't have to apologize to the likes of us. Besides they're still paying for the hub here. Their hub. Delta may be funneling millions of people into our airport from other cities, but at least two-thirds of them never leave the airport. They're Delta's customers, not Cincinnati's.

Delta pumps about four hundred, thirty-nine million dollars into our economy every year. I'm grateful. I'm also glad Procter & Gamble keeps its international headquarters here. But I don't expect to pay more for a bar of Ivory soap than somebody in Louisville.

Why is a ticket out of Cincinnati more expensive than out of Columbus? Unions? Deregulation? Debt service? Market share? Frills? Here's why I think it is:

Because they can.

— October, 1995

UFO UPDATE:
DRIVE CAREFULLY

NOW, I ALREADY know that I am not one of those people who excels at "thinking outside the box." Frankly, if the box was good enough for our parents, I say it should be good enough for us. You just can't be too careful when it comes to new ideas. I have only recently allowed myself to believe in the existence of fat-free cookies.

But it appears that there is something mysterious at work out there. Otherwise, how can we explain goatees, the stock market and Courtney Love?

So I went to a UFO support group meeting.

Apparently there have been strange sightings all over the place. For instance, a glowing red object was reported by people in the Middletown and Carlisle area. Now, I don't know about you, but I see glowing red lights all the time and I choose to ignore them. This is probably why my car ran out of gas twice last year.

Anyway, a man named Bode Gibbs described the Middletown phenomenon as round, glowing, with red lights and said the object twice appeared to dump a "ball of burning liquid." This sounds exactly like what happened to Harvey Fierstein in the movie Independence Day, except that the wall of burning liquid was lethal. Mr. Gibbs said he was reluctant to report the sighting because of his position as a leader of a Star Trek fan club.

Right. You can't be too careful.

The police in Middletown, who received about three hundred calls, say they think pranksters are responsible. Ditto for the crop circle that showed up in a farmer's field in northwestern Ohio. Hundreds of people visited the site. Some were looking for evidence that the ninety-three-foot mashed, perfectly formed circle was caused by the landing of a vehicle from outer space. The rest were looking for sweet corn.

John Timmerman, who lives nearby and studies UFOs, says he knows how the pranksters did it, but won't tell because he's afraid of copycats. This would, he said, taint his UFO research.

Right. You can't be too careful.

Likewise, I went into my own research with great care and some skepticism. I probably did not believe I was going to meet anybody who had been abducted by aliens. About the best I thought I could do would be to meet someone who honestly thinks they've been abducted by aliens.

Evidence presented by people at the meeting was subtle. Nobody had pictures or ET's autograph or even artifacts that read, "Mom was abducted by aliens and all I got was a lousy T-shirt." Most of it was more reports of flashing lights. But one woman described an experience that convinced her aliens were "among us."

She said she was riding along in her car when suddenly she discovered that the sleeves of her blouse were too tight. I guess she thought that they'd beamed her up and when they replaced her, their calibrations were a little off.

Not wanting to be the bearer of sad tidings, I did not tell her that every middle-aged woman suddenly discovers that the sleeves of her blouse are too tight. Most of us do not complain because we know that without sleeves, if we attempt a friendly wave of spontaneous applause, we will be flogged to death by our own upper arms.

So, "get real" is what I wanted to say to her. But I was too polite.

The general consensus seemed to be that creatures from outer space visit all the time, but our government keeps this information from us. The U.S. government, if I may say so, leaks like a sieve. Just ask the Clintons. Or the Reagans. If the government was going to keep a secret, why not the one about J. Edgar Hoover in an evening gown?

I confided some of my reservations to a member of the UFO support group. She was disappointed by my attitude. "Maybe if you had a more open mind, you might learn something," she said. "If we can't trust you, we won't tell you some of the really bizarre things we know."

Right. You can't be too careful.

— *July, 1996*

Thanks, Ralph, For The Moving Violation

RALPH NADER PROBABLY isn't losing any sleep over it, but I have never forgiven him for ruining the Corvair.

His *Unsafe at any Speed* was a best-seller, and the next thing you know, Ralph Nader is America's foremost consumer advocate and the Corvair is America's foremost death trap.

He had his reasons for trashing the Corvair, although I can't remember what they were. All I know is that my father picked out that car for me, and he would never have put me in anything that was dangerous. (Dad really thought the most dangerous vehicles for girl children were the ones that were parked.)

My Corvair, a nineteen sixty-six Monza, started every morning, and was so handsome that it was stolen twice. I loved that car.

These days, the country suffers from road rage and a love affair with four-wheel-drive hogs, driven by people who neither live on ranches nor drive through blizzards. They make a statement: This driver has a lot of money and thinks minivans are dorky.

My Corvair said it did not promise to be safe at any speed, but it would start in the morning and sip gasoline. And look cute.

Maybe my memories of this car are so fond because it

took me to drive-in movies. It hauled my laundry home from college. The Supremes and the Beach Boys sang to me in that car.

I understand that my little car was a casualty of Ralph Nader's campaign for auto safety, and I'm better off with air bags and shoulder restraints and seatbelts. I don't even mind that it's no longer my choice whether to use them. He has moved on to olestra and tort reform and corporate welfare.

After thirty years in the limelight with some of the most powerful enemies in the country, he has been untouched by scandal and unmoved by pressure. So, I probably have to admire him.

But I just wish he'd left the Corvair alone.

— July, 1997

At Last, The Truth About Traffic Delays

TO ALL MY fellow east-siders, I would like to say that I am sincerely sorry. Construction delays on I-71 are all my personal, miserable fault.

This is a lifelong curse, and anybody who went to Shawnee Elementary School in Lima, Ohio, during the nineteen fifties can tell you that the worst place to be at lunchtime was in the cafeteria line behind me. The ladies in hairnets would run out of macaroni and cheese or there would be a toxic Jell-O spill. Or something. But anyway, the line would grind to a halt.

Later on, the curse followed me to banks and the grocery check-out lanes. It might be a price check, or somebody with a bag of pennies, but the common denominator was always me. I was right behind them.

Recently, I visited Florida, and as I drove to the airport, I wondered how many travelers would be late to their destinations courtesy of me. At the convenient, curbside luggage check-in, I was behind a potential terrorist, about eighty-five years old, who could not locate her picture ID. Or, indeed, her purse. Or her daughter-in-law. Then she couldn't find a quarter for the baggage handler.

We were ticketed aboard an airline that I will not name because the following events are really not their fault. They are trying very hard to be the airline of our dreams, and they cannot help it if they have to pay for a big new terminal. And if it costs us a little more for that convenience, I feel certain that their peanuts, which are of superior quality, will more than compensate for the extra cost of flying this particular airline out of Cincinnati.

So, let me emphasize this: This is not the fault of the airline. The weather was windy and snowy, and on top of that, they were afflicted by the Pulfer Curse.

First, a problem in Atlanta — scuttlebutt in the waiting area was that it was either the weather or the President getting a haircut — that delayed the flight. This gave the agents at the gate plenty of time to negotiate with the overflow of passengers. The flight had been overbooked. Who knew that all these people would really want to fly south in February?

Periodic announcements extended the delay a little at a time, so everybody was scared to leave the boarding area, even though we knew that it was dinner time and we were about to board the Peanuts R Us evening flight.

Except for the people in first class — who we can assume were dining on quail and wild rice and laughing up their Turnbull & Asser sleeves at people in coach — everybody was starved. A woman on one side of me offered to trade her Ferragamo shoes for my Country Store Popcorn.

No deal.

When we arrived in Atlanta, we had to run to catch our connecting flight. You will not be surprised to learn that the baggage handlers did not run as fast as we did. So when we arrived in Florida, we had that most woeful of traveling experiences — filling out the Lost Baggage Claim.

I felt terrible, but at least these people united by the Pulfer Curse in the Lost Baggage Waiting Room, were not my neighbors.

A few years ago, I moved to Mariemont, and work began on Wooster Pike. This lasted for years. Until I moved to Hyde Park and started bragging about getting downtown in eight minutes. Then it was only a matter of time until the talk began in earnest about construction on I-71. So, here we are today. Orange barrels as far as the eye can see.

If you have been driving around like a rat in a maze hoping to find a route downtown, I have some advice for you. Get yourself a car phone. This way, you will look important and busy to your fellow commuters. (You'll really be trying to be the seventh caller to Radio Station JACR so that you can win tickets to various cultural events such as Pearl Jam concerts or mud wrestling.)

You can also use the phone to call for a pizza in case you get behind me at dinnertime.

— March, 1996

DIVERSITY TRAINING

RIDE THE BUS. You'll get more than a cheap trip home.

My personal favorite is the Madisonville, Number Eleven, which has a nice assortment of Cincinnati's citizens. Diversity, we like to call it. Black and white. Young and old. Well-off and not so well-off, if we knew each other well enough to exchange this kind of information. Blue collar and white collar and T-shirt collar.

The other night it was crowded. Full. You were lucky to get a seat. I got one next to a woman of ample proportions. So we were just a little more, shall we say, overlapping, than I actually like to be. Halfway through the trip, this woman moved from the seat next to me to stand in the aisle. She explained that she wanted to make sure that "she has a seat." She was an old woman, leaning heavily on a cane, wearing a fake leopard coat and clutching a plastic shopping bag with a Stouffer's dinner, among other personal items.

The old woman was white, if that makes any difference to you. The woman who gave up her seat was black. And young.

The old woman asked the bus driver if he would stop at her street, which was not officially a bus stop. He certainly would. He stopped, and she moved painfully down the steps, juggling her bag and her cane. The bus driver said, "You just take your time, ma'am. We are not in any hurry here."

The people in the front of the bus winced as she struggled, ready to help. But not too soon. Trying not to look as though they were watching. She was doing this by herself. She made it.

We smiled at each other. We were young and old and black and white. If this matters to you.

— *WVXU radio, May, 1997*

DREAM TRIP FROM
FRIENDLY STRANGERS

MY BAGS ARE packed, and I am just waiting around to see who wants to send me on a vacation next. What have I done to deserve this attention? I wish I knew.

First, a notice from Florida Travel Network arrived announcing that I am the "confirmed recipient of our spectacular eight-day, seven-night fantasy holiday" to Florida and the Caribbean. These people want to sent me on a really fancy trip beginning in Orlando, home of Mickey and Goofy, then on to a cruise in the Bahamas. Not to mention "three sensational nights in Fort Lauderdale."

And I have never met them in my life.

You may be thinking this is some sort of come-on, but I could tell it was a legitimately wonderful prize because they were "delighted to advise me via FIRST CLASS MAIL." Would they waste a thirty-two-cent stamp on the likes of me unless there was something very special at stake?

I think not.

Not to brag, but I think they choose people of influence who will tell their wealthy friends about all the fun. In fact, it says this is "to promote tourism to Florida and the Bahamas." Sounds like a good cause, and I'd like to do my part. Besides, maybe I'll get to aerobicize with Kathie Lee and Frank Gifford.

I dialed the convenient eight-hundred number, and Steve answered. "Are you ready to hear about your exciting trip?" he asked.

Well, who wouldn't be?

First stop, Orlando. "Wait a minute. How do I get to Orlando?" I asked.

Steve explained that of course I would be responsible for my own transportation to Florida. Well, of course.

I didn't want to appear greedy, but what about tickets to

Walt Disney World, Universal Studios and Sea World? "What do you do when you get to Orlando is completely up to you," Steve said. "But we do supply brochures. In color."

He was beginning to sound peeved.

Then on to Fort Lauderdale, where after "three sensational nights at the beautiful Sunrise Hilton" comes the cruise. Geez. I must have been born under a star.

Steve mentioned a ninety-nine-dollar-per-person "docking fee." It was too confusing for us, so Steve put his supervisor, Bart, on the phone. Bart explained that this is "something that goes directly to the government and you have to pay it, unless you're a good swimmer. Heh. Heh."

Poor Steve is probably beginning to suspect that I am not the high-roller he is accustomed to booking on these promotional gigs, and he tells me that there's a daily "user fee" of nine to eleven dollars per person and there may be charges for maid service and phones and pools, etc.

So, anyway, now I'm going to hear about the Bahamas cruise. "How long is this cruise, Steve."

"You're on the ship about six to eight hours, each way," Steve says. So, I guess I'll have to put a racing stripe on my fork if I want to get the most out of the "Las Vegas-style shows, non-stop casino action and endless meals."

The ship deposits merrymakers for "three sunny days and two tranquil nights on this island paradise, enjoying golf, duty-free shopping, deep-sea fishing." This is a la carte, of course.

Of course. But I'm assuming I will be getting those color brochures.

No kidding now, Steve, what will all this cost me? "Only two hundred, forty-nine dollars per person." I have to decide now because (and I could tell that he felt bad about this) he's only allowed to authorize one phone call per household, and the offer will expire when I hang up. So, unfortunately I can't check with my husband or any other travel agents before I decide.

"Steve, you know the information I got in the mail makes it sound like this is a free trip." He says only "people who are kind of ignorant think it's free."

I think maybe this job has soured him a little bit on human nature. For instance, he told me that sometimes when he tells people about the two hundred, forty-nine dollars, they'll say they don't have the money. He tells them that they can use their Visa or Mastercard.

"And some of them say they don't have one," he says disgustedly. "And we know they're lying. That's how we got their name. You just can't trust anybody."

Well, Steve, I'm sorry to hear that.

— *March, 1996*

Nine

CONTEMPLATING
MIDDLE-AGED NAVELS

"With love and security — and
an occasional ice cream bar —
our children will turn out
like Dick and Jane."
                    —*Captain Kangaroo*

WHO'S AFRAID OF THE DEMOGRAPHIC PIG?

BABY BOOMERS ARE turning fifty. One every seven and a half seconds for the next decade. Expect that we will be utterly fascinated by ourselves as usual.

Look for plenty of riveting discussions about menopause and prostates and dental implants. And plenty of ads for Miracle Ear and bifocals and hair dye and Rogaine. Couples will probably give each other designer blood-pressure cuffs for special occasions. I only wish I had the stewed-prune-and-bran concession for this decade.

We have been described as sort of a demographic pig working our way through the python. But I think that's unkind, don't you? We can't help it that almost from birth we've been the target of somebody trying to sell us something.

Here's something I wish we could buy: There's nothing wrong with getting old.

I'm not sure how chummy I'll be with my own wrinkles, but I don't think I want to have all the life nipped and tucked out of my face either. I sure don't want to end my life looking startled and perpetually alert with a mouth like an open purse.

It will be interesting to see, as we Boomers age, what we'll choose to do. And how we'll choose to look. Will our ears get bigger and our noses longer and our eyelids droopier? Or will we keep carving away at them?

Just as we thought we invented sex during the sixties and divorce during the seventies, we are not going to be discovering age spots and jowls. I wonder if we'll keep them.

There are seventy-six million of us and we've been trained to expect that whatever we want will be waiting for us. So, will it be a festival of wrinkles? A celebration of cellulite?

Or drive-through cosmetic surgery and wrinkle cream by the vat?

— *WVXU, January, 1995*

LAUGHING ALL THE WAY
TO GEEZERHOOD

WE CALL OURSELVES the Bridge Club, although we don't play cards. We don't have dues, rules or a superior attitude toward people who are not members. We call ourselves the Bridge Club because we think that sounds more elegant than "a bunch of women getting together to eat too much and laugh."

Some of us are married and some of us are not. The ones who are married don't complain about their husbands, and the ones who are single don't complain about men and their failure to commit. All of us work, but none of us is politically correct enough to add "outside the home" when we say so.

When we first knew each other, we were all in our late

twenties and early thirties, and our idea of a racy evening was ogling the bag boys at Kroger. We did not discuss our digestion. Or our cholesterol. Or trophy wives. Or hot flashes.

But now the Bridge Club has come of age. Middle Age. That is, if we're all planning to live to be one hundred.

This could be the ideal time for a pep talk from Mary-Lou Weisman, author of My Middle-Aged Baby Book: A record of Milestones, Millstones and Gallstones. A free-lance writer, she swears she just tossed this one off for fun. "If I'd known it was going to be a hit, I'd have written a more expensive book."

True, it's only twelve dollars and ninety-five cents, but about twenty-eight million baby boomers will have a fiftieth birthday over the next decade. This sounds like a chance to give them something more fun than a gift certificate for a truss or estrogen pills. Modeled after the baby books that our moms kept for us, it lists such watershed events as "buys first jeans with elastic waist" and "stops wearing Spandex."

Just ahead of the baby boom herself, Weisman is fifty-eight and calls herself simply a grown-up. Middle age, according to her, is when you're over forty. Hmmm. Could you be a little more specific?

"If you've begun to wonder why your gums recede, if you have Tums in your pocket and Mylanta in your drawer, and if you have your proctologist's phone number on speed dial, you've reached middle age."

Oh. I'm sorry I asked.

Like its author, Middle-Aged Baby Book is funny and thin but unmistakably substantial. It's an invitation to laugh our way to old age, reassurance that we're not alone and the suggestion that there is some very good time left.

Maybe this is a club we'd all like to join, no matter what it's called.

— *May, 1996*

DICK AND JANE GROWN UP, IN THERAPY

MY FIRST-GRADE teacher once scraped mud off my new saddle shoes with a Popsicle stick after I said my dear, gentle mother would "kill me" when she saw them. Sympathetic but strict, Mrs. Winegardner carried a pitch pipe, wore sensible shoes and kept her hankie in her brassiere. We carefully averted our eyes when she was searching for it.

It was an innocent time.

We were growing up with Smith Brothers cough drops, which were really candy in disguise; Howdy Doody, who was a freckled wooden boy; and, of course, Dick and Jane, the brother and sister who taught us all to read.

I know that I speak for Dick and Jane when I say they would be shocked to know they have become "icons of the American culture." A new book by Carole Kismaric and Marvin Heiferman, *Growing Up with Dick and Jane*, has taken Dick and Jane and Sally and Father and Mother — even Spot,

Puff and Tim — and analyzed them nearly beyond recognition.

Bob Keeshan, the former Captain Kangaroo and the first Clarabell Clown on the *Howdy Doody Show* wrote the preface:

"With love and security — and an occasional ice cream bar — our children will turn out like Dick and Jane. I'll let you in on a secret. The Dicks and Janes of this world grow into happy human beings."

As well they might, Captain.

Dick, in one of several beautiful illustrations, poses sturdily, hands in his pockets, looking directly off the page, He is, according to the authors, "Master of a little world that stretches from his screen door, across the green lawn to a white picket fence."

When Dick says "Look," everybody does.

Meanwhile Jane is "smart and down-to-earth. She hovers on the outskirts of the action — always there if someone needs her." And, by the way, this child is a major clotheshorse. According to the book, she traveled through her forty-year career wearing at least two hundred different ensembles, always dresses.

She wore a spotless little dress to ride a pony, and "she's so neat that even Spot and Puff know not to jump on her." Spot and Puff were the family pets, a perky springer spaniel and tiny orange kitten. They are completely housebroken.

Sally is the baby, cute, very cute. Mother is a whirlwind

of cooking, cleaning and sewing. She never has PMS or a bad-hair day. Father is young, handsome, tall and, we may assume, prosperous.

This family has everything but a last name.

Well, no wonder we postwar babies started drinking and taking drugs. No wonder so many of us are in therapy. Reality must have been a terrible disappointment for us. Would we have been better off if we'd been reading books such as *Heather Has Two Mommies*? I don't know, but I think it's worth discussing.

I hope everybody notices that our kids are not getting their view of life exclusively from the shelves of their school libraries. When they are assigned to read a book at school, at least a teacher is available to help them understand things they find disturbing. Nobody is writing *Cliff Notes* for the learning experience of MTV or the mall.

Some parents at Lakota High School want to protect their children from the writing of Maya Angelou. (The best way, of course, would be to demand that they read it.) *I Know Why the Caged Bird Sings*, which contains a vivid description of the rape of an eight-year-old girl, was challenged as unfit to be required reading for high school kids.

I happen to have the outrageous view that parents have a right — actually, an obligation — to take an interest in their children's schooling, including their books. I don't consider it censorship to debate the decisions of teachers, librarians and administrators.

After all, don't we want the best possible education for our children? Don't we want to prepare them as best we can to cope with the world that awaits? Dick was never forced to join a gang. Nobody offered heroin to Jane on the playground.

It was, however, an innocent time.

— *September, 1996*

DAD'S GARDEN: A SUBURBAN TALE OF PLENTY

MY DAD USED to plant a wonderful garden. Nice neat rows, straight as an arrow. Then he would lose interest.

The details fell to my mother. Mom did the weeding and watering and staked up the vines with old nylon stockings. Suburbanites, not farmers, we never had a big garden, but it was amazingly fruitful. We used to say that Dad had a green thumb. We did not say that with enthusiasm.

My brothers and I could never figure out how he chose his crops. There was, for instance, the Year of the Gourds. I don't know how much you know about gourds, but they are not good for anything. They're billed as decorative, but it would be a desperate decor, if you ask me, that would be improved by a gourd.

You can't eat them, and although the seed packet said that they often are used for vessels and utensils, we never stumbled upon an occasion that seemed to call for chips and onion dip out of a gourd. Improperly handled, the instructions said, they might be poisonous. Hollowing them out to make a tea set sounded highly improper to us. So we picked them, and put them in a dry place. "Waste not, want not" is probably on our family crest.

We had hundreds of gourds, ugly and warty-looking. We tried to give them away, but nobody else wanted them either. Finally, we started hiding them in the cars of visitors. People learned to look in the back seat before they left.

"Oh, you are too kind," they'd say. "We'll never, uh, use all these beautiful gourds." The only useful thing about the gourds was that they were good practice for the yellow wax beans and, the following year, the bread-and-butter pickles.

The Great Yellow Wax Bean Harvest had a promising start. At least they were edible. Anything you can do with green beans, you can do with yellow wax beans. Of course, they just don't taste as good as green beans, and we asked Dad why he chose the yellow ones.

"I like them," he said.

We took yellow wax beans to every imaginable covered-dish event. Cooked with ham. With onions. With mushroom soup. We combined them with just about everything except gourds. We even took them to the bereaved. I'm not proud of this, but none of us could bear to just throw them away.

The following year when we saw him looking through seed catalogs, we begged, "Please, Dad, can't you plant something we like this year?" He looked offended as though he hadn't noticed that we were the scourge of the casserole patrol. As though he hadn't noticed that everybody who came to our house that summer locked their cars as soon as they pulled into the driveway.

"How about cucumbers?" he said.

"How about tomatoes? Or corn on the cob?" we countered.

The thing about cucumbers, Dad said, is that they are really pickles. My mom pointed out that they don't just grow up to be pickles. Somebody has to encourage them, she said desperately.

It was too late. The seeds were in the ground.

We love our mother, and we tried to eat as many cucumbers as we could. We peddled them by the bushel to friends and neighbors, who were relieved to see that we were not trying to palm off gourds or yellow wax beans.

We just couldn't keep ahead of the crop. My mother finally called us together and said we would have to take stronger measures. We would have to make pickles. As the family bookworm, I was sent to the library to read up on botulism.

For a whole week, my mother made something called bread-and-butter pickles from a recipe my dad's mom gave her. Grandma swore that my dad loved them.

Nobody loved them, including my dad. But our friends were very good about opening their hearts (and their cars) to this new crop. We believe they did if for the Mason jars, which cost a fortune.

My father died last year. This is the first harvest without him. We all cope with grief in different, often trivial ways. Myself, I planted a garden.

And my friends have learned to look before they sit in the back seats of their cars.

— *September, 1996*

THE HIGH-FAT, LOW-TECH DIET

DO YOU FEEL in need of fresh air? Would you like to go someplace with your family where you don't have to walk through a metal detector? Have you just about had it with tofu and fake fat and noodles that are called pasta? Are you looking for a little reassurance that America, as you know it, has not been completely ruined by lunatics?

Go to a county fair. You'll feel better immediately.

Any county fair will do, but the best ones are far from city traffic and urban amusements. Look for one where the big attractions are still Four-H kids with cows and an innocence that can produce an adolescent girl proud to be called Pork Queen. Try to find one where they give a blue ribbon for the best apron.

If you see a bank of video games and corporate sponsors and people wearing topsiders and lime green pants, you are in the wrong place. You should be seeing old boots with real mud and belt buckles the size of dinner plates.

The nose rings are on the cattle.

You want to look for truck and tractor pulls, demolition derbies, flower shows, mountain clog dancers and livestock sales. There should be pony rides and a Ferris wheel and a dunking booth. Competition for the best canned beans should be fierce. But there is no competition for parking.

For one dollar you can leave your car all day in the shade at the fairgrounds north of Hamilton. The young man who directed me to my space in the grass allowed enough room on either side for me to open my door without dinging the car on either side. He held my purse while I looked for my sunglasses.

For another dollar, I bought an enormous cloud of pink cotton candy, which looked just exactly like Tammy Faye Baker's hair on a good day. Never mind that two hours earlier, in another life, I insisted that the waiter deliver my salad with the dressing on the side.

There's something wonderfully liberating about eating a funnel cake in public and standing in line to buy something called "fried dough." Nothing had labels on the side with nagging reminders about sodium and potassium. No mention was made of fat grams, and I think we can assume that anything you eat while walking down a midway has no socially or nutritionally redeeming value.

That's the point. Just about the most dangerous experience you'll have at a county fair is cholesterol overload. Or a sugar high. If you want to pet the lambs, you don't have to check first to see whether there are razor blades hidden in the wool. The bunnies do not have explosives in their ears. You do not have to pay extra to see sheep shearing.

No one is smoking dope in the audience at the grandstand during the horse show or the harness racing. Politicians in shirt sleeves give away refrigerator magnets and note paper and rulers. But they don't make you listen to any speeches or ask for money. They don't even try to kiss your baby. It's too hot, and there are no TV cameras.

The big police presence at the Butler County Fair was a sheriff's department tent with Officer Bob and his horse. No guns were drawn, and I scored another refrigerator magnet.

If somebody jostles you while you're trying to win a hat at the dart games, they'll apologize and offer to buy a round of darts. I am not kidding. You can usually toss a ring and, for about ten times what it would cost in a store, win a two-liter bottle of Coke. I never did see a salad bar.

Maybe you'd just like your kids to see "the other white meat" on the hoof. Or meet Officer Bob's horse. Maybe you'd simply like to remember what it felt like to be safe. Fried dough, corn dogs, cotton candy and French waffles with powdered sugar and a contest to see who made the best apron may not be conventional medicine. But it's a lot cheaper than Prozac.

And it feels a lot better than giving up.

— *July, 1996*

CORNY SIGNS TELL US
WHERE WE'VE BEEN

SO THEY'RE PLANNING to bring back the Burma-Shave signs for us Baby Boomers, are they?

Within this vale

Of toil

And sin

Your head grows bald

But not your chin.

Of course, there will be a few modern improvements. Instead of red-and-white wooden signs, maintained along back roads by farmers for five dollars a year and a free box of shaving cream, thirty-second television commercials were produced by media experts with omigod fees.

Instead of Grace Odell hopping up in the middle of the night with a flashlight and a pencil and paper to record her husband's latest rhyming brainstorm, there is a senior vice president for consumer and personal products at American Safety Razor, which bought the brand from Philip Morris, which bought if from the Odells.

A brand identity consultant. Focus groups. Account supervisions. Many, many billable hours. A one-and-a-half-million-dollar campaign.

The TV spots show a man in his mid-fifties driving a nineteen fifty-eight Corvette. Next to him is his decade-younger trophy wife. Passing a set of Burma-Shave signs, they are apparently overcome with lust. Next, the viewer sees a parked car, doors open, the couple presumably off-camera ripping off their clothes and using the shaving cream for heaven only knows what.

We know you.

Really love

That gal

But use both hands

For driving, pal.

Allan Odell wrote most of the rhymes, according to James Delaney, who produced a video account of the Odell family and their "funny little idea." Burma-Vita employed thirty-five people. Eight trucks in the company "fleet" ferried signs to forty-five of the forty-eight states between nineteen twenty-six and nineteen sixty-three, when Philip Morris yanked them.

Mr. Odell, who died in nineteen ninety, was a "wonderfully whimsical man."

The bearded lady

Tried a jar

Now she's a

Famous movie star.

"He had the idea advertising should be something you could laugh at," Grace Odell says. So the Odells laughed themselves right into second-place sales, after Barbasol.

When the stork

Delivers a boy

The whole

Darn company
Jumps for joy.

As if to prove that if you could sell shaving cream, you could sell anything, the company peddled war bonds.

Maybe you can't
Shoulder a gun
But you can shoulder
the cost of one.

The signs have disappeared from their natural habitat — deserted two-lane country roads — but are preserved in fancier places, including the Smithsonian Institution. The growth in the nineteen sixties of interstate highways was their downfall. Six signs, placed one hundred feet apart, were made to be read at speeds of thirty-five miles an hour. By people who would take the time to look, and who could smile and drive at the same time.

Here's a modest suggestion. Dump the TV campaign with the couple panting in the bushes. Bring back the red and white signs with Allan Odell's wry couplets. Put them on every tenth orange barrel.

These little signs
Have come of age
They'll be the
Cure for our
Road rage.

— *July, 1997*

140

Ten

I BEG TO DIFFER

*"To describe the beating
of egg whites is almost as
cheeky as advising how
to lead a happy life."*
— The Joy of Cooking

ARE MICKEY AND MINNIE DANGEROUS?

NO WONDER THE Southern Baptists decided to boycott Disney. Maybe this will bring some attention to the danger this company poses to the morals of our children.

A resolution, passed by twelve hundred delegates to the Baptists' convention, urges the fifteen million members of the nation's largest Protestant denomination to take action against Disney's "anti-Christian and anti-family direction." They want to avenge "immoral ideologies and practices."

They could start with Minnie Mouse. If I've seen that hussy's underpants once, I've seen them a thousand times. And have you noticed the open-toed shoes? I think we all know what these are called. And why.

How about Snow White? You can't tell me that there wasn't something between her and Sneezy. Heigh-ho, heigh-ho indeed. I've seen the inside of that dwarf love nest, and Doc is bunking just a little too close to Bashful to suit me.

Goofy clearly has been addled by drugs and alcohol, and I'd like somebody to explain to me how Scrooge McDuck has made his fortune. I suspect the rackets — prostitution and gambling. Huey, Dewey and Louie probably are his numbers runners. Is it my imagination, or are those beepers under their feathers?

And who does Donald Duck think he's fooling in his prissy little sailor hat and middy blouse with no pants. That sicko.

This looks like a chance for a mass book burning, starting with the Little Golden Ones. Put the Lion King and the Little Mermaid videos in a Hefty bag and bid good-bye to Bill Nye, the Science Guy, another Disney shill.

The real target, of course, is not Minnie Mouse, but the openly gay Ellen DeGeneres, whose eponymous show is on Disney's ABC. The company's policy of providing medical benefits to same-sex couples is damned as "gay-friendly." That seems a peculiarly hard stance, considering that this country has thirty-seven million people who have no health coverage at all. This policy must cost Disney a fortune. I suppose that is kind of friendly.

C'mon, Baptists, you can find a more worthy enemy than Disney. If you want to go after a cartoon character, how about Joe Camel? What about what's happening to our heterosexual teen-age girls? Babies. Lots of babies. According to the Family and Children First Action Team, about eighty percent of all poverty has been linked to teen pregnancies.

This is not caused by homosexuals.

The Southern Baptists have millions of members scattered in communities all over the country. I know plenty of them, and they're decent and energetic people. Their impact can be mighty. How about targeting drugs? Or guns?

I mean no disrespect. In fact, the good that a group like this one can accomplish is awe-inspiring. But surely this church can find more dangerous enemies than Mickey and Minnie. Surely their robust interest in the family can find a better target than a company that spends millions of dollars on medical benefits to people who might otherwise be shut out and ignored. Or supported by taxpayers.

When you think about it, what the Southern Baptists are asking is that Disney withdraw somebody's access to health care. This boycott is not really funny. It's goofy.

And it's, well, kind of immoral.

— *June, 1997*

THE TEACHER AS FAT CAT

EXCUSE ME FOR saying so because I enjoy blood and gore as much as the next person, but I think the scariest story lately is the one about public schools.

Kids are dropping out in record numbers, and guess who is to blame? Their teachers. Not their parents. Not crime. Not drugs. Not poverty. Their teachers, especially their teachers' unions.

Bob Dole says Bob Dole thinks the unions have "run our public schools into the ground."

Think of it. Fat-cat teachers who have the country in, as Mr. Dole puts it, their "vicelike grip." There must be shrieks of laughter out there from all the powerful, overpaid teachers eating Grey Poupon from the backseats of their limos. Teachers' country clubs must be planning to raise their greens fees.

Remember when we were in school? When we got in trouble there, it would not have occurred to us to take a

144

swing at our teacher. Teachers used to send us to the office for chewing gum. Now our teachers have to walk through metal detectors to get to class.

How many kids have two parents showing up for teacher conferences? Or one parent, for that matter? How many own a gun? How many are carrying beepers? How many have not had breakfast before they leave home? How many belong to a gang? How many students have to drop their children off at a day-care center before they go to school?

In short, what kind of student do we deliver to the classroom? How ready are they to learn? And why would we expect that our teachers can cure pregnancy, drugs and poverty during algebra class? And, excuse me for saying so, because I enjoy blaming somebody else as much as the next person, but it's not the fault of teachers that our children are in trouble.

It's our fault.

— *National Public Radio,*
August, 1996

THE ROMANCE OF STEALING AND CONFESSING

CONFESSION IS GOOD for the soul. Now, let's see what it will do for book sales.

Romance novelist Janet Daily, who should not be confused with an actual author, has admitted that she borrowed from the work of her rival Nora Roberts. Ms. Roberts has issued a statement warning darkly that the plagiarism discovered so far is "only the tip of the iceberg."

Well, I should think so.

For instance, who owns the rights to *heaving* and *throbbing*? And what creative mind first decided that every hero should be chiseled and bronzed? Unless, of course, he is rugged with the beginnings of a five o'clock shadow. But they all have pecs like Fabio's and are big. Tall. Big and tall. And not bald.

Their names sound like race horses or small towns in New England. Whose idea was it to name all the men Devon and Hunter and Roarke and Kane and Hawk? What about Charlie? Or Bud? The women are Eden and Jemma and Cady, who sometimes have a streak of independence. They all have unruly long locks, sometimes tangled, but never trimmed into a becoming pixie.

Who first decided to use the phrase *secret place*, when *down there* was perfectly serviceable?

If Mrs. Dailey's disclosure about the origins of her nineteen ninety-six book, *Notorious*, sells more copies of it, maybe all imitators will confess. This would save the book police the tedium of looking for larceny in the gezillion romance novels on the market and in every garage sale in America.

It's not easy to spot a theft. "Whatever skill he had, whatever patience he's developed, he would use tonight," reads a passage in Nora Roberts' book, *Sweet Revenge*. Mrs. Daily said she swiped that passage for *Notorious*, where we learn that "Tonight demanded all the skill and patience he possessed."

This is just one flagrant example. Ms. Roberts said she is poring over other books by Mrs. Dailey hoping to bring "an end to this disturbing pattern in a way that best serves the interests of the writing community."

Not to mention the reading community.

"I can only apologize to Nora, whom I've considered a friend, and to my readers for any pain or embarrassment my conduct has caused," Mrs. Daily said.

Really, I think this woman is being too hard on herself. Everybody's doing it, not just romance novelists.

Take Martha Stewart. Do you think she came up with the idea of whipping egg whites into peaks? If so, I'll refer you to pages five hundred forty-four to forty-five of *The Joy of Cooking* by Irma S. Rombauer and Marion Rombauer Becker. "To describe the beating of egg whites is almost as cheeky as advising how to lead a happy life." Nonetheless, they advise that eggs be beaten until they "stand in peaks that are firm, but still soft."

Aha. And this was written years before *The Martha Stewart Cookbook* told us on page five hundred ninety-four to whip our egg whites "until soft peaks form." Clearly, the Rombauers also inspired Julia Child, generally beloved even though she suffers from vocal disharmony and has been, for the most part, too tall. On page two hundred ninety of *In Julia's Kitchen with*

Master Chefs, she advises readers to whip eggs into — you guessed it — "soft peaks."

This must be the culinary equivalent of "greedy mouths" and "milky white breasts."

Anyway, now that Janet Dailey has been featured on national television and in newspapers all over the country, I think we can look forward to a flurry of contrition from writers. Maybe even from painters and musicians.

Just in case confessing is good for the career, I stole the description of Julia Child from my friend Frank Shue, who is retired and has nothing better to do than think of impolite things to say. I sincerely hope that my coming clean about this matter will result in an invitation from Oprah and a serious conversation with Stone Phillips.

— August, 1997

HONK IF YOU'RE A BIGOT

IT'S HARD TO decide which side to take in the matter of private clubs. On the one hand, most of us deplore race and gender discrimination. At least publicly. On the other hand, why not encourage bigots to clump together so it will be easier to identify them? And avoid them. And refuse to help them prosper.

In fact, maybe we should insist that they not only hang out together, but wear badges: "I refuse to golf with women,

Jews or people of color." Or maybe a bumper sticker. Yes, that would be even better. Then after you have left the club, you can let the whole world know exactly where you stand.

Bills to ban race and gender discrimination at private clubs have been proposed in several states. Michigan and Minnesota have passed such bills. One was introduced in Ohio. For the fourth time.

The Ohio legislator who sponsors the bill says it's an economic issue. That private clubs often are the location for business deals. So, we need another bumper sticker: "I prefer to do business exclusively with white men who golf."

Instead of insisting that country clubs open their men's grill rooms to women, maybe men could just wear T-shirts that say "I refuse to eat with women." Then their wives and daughters and female employees could make sure the guys never have to relax their dining standards outside the club.

Nobody has to join a country club. We're not guaranteed life, liberty and the pursuit of golf, although twenty-five million Americans have chosen to take up this aggravating sport. Of those, twenty-one percent are women. Do you suppose Coca-Cola would ignore twenty-one percent of cola drinkers? What if women who golf would join only clubs that allow them full privileges? What if Tiger Woods refused to play at clubs with restrictive policies?

It seems to me that the others would have a lot of leftover bumper stickers.

— *WVXU radio, July, 1997*

We Can Refuse To Be Hustled

YOU KNOW THAT "gawker's lag" you see after a big highway accident? Traffic slows and clogs while passing motorists try to catch a glimpse of gore. I've never understood why anybody would enjoy seeing someone in a body bag or gushing blood.

If I were the first one there and could do anything useful, I like to believe I would not be too squeamish to jump out of my car to help. But if a crowd was already there, including people trained to handle such emergencies, I'd stay out of the way.

And I wouldn't look.

When I notice somebody curbing his dog — even though it is my perfect right as a citizen to inspect the scene and glower if I see no evidence of an immediate cleanup — I don't watch. If I want to be disgusted to death, I'll go to New York and get somebody to throw up on my shoes in the subway.

Then there are your garden-variety flashers. Most women know that part of their thrill is our reaction. If we don't appear to notice, it takes all the fun out of it for them.

These are all the reasons I avoid press conferences convened by Larry Flynt. Sanitized and sanctified by Hollywood, he has come back to spit in our eye. Or probably another version would be that he has come to lift the veil of oppression from the eyes of people starved for the sight of a woman in handcuffs.

But I don't have to look. So I exercise my right to stay away.

"I really do care about the First Amendment," Mr. Flynt says. And I believe he is sincere about that. It has made him a very wealthy man. And I think that lurking inside that born-again crusader is the original businessman and hustler.

He won't pass out free copies of his magazine indefinitely. Eventually he will try to sell his junk. Here. If it's illegal, it will be settled in court. He has plenty of lawyers, and he has rights.

And we have the right to look away.

— *March, 1997*

IS IT LOVE, OR JUST POSTAL ATTRACTION?

MAYBE I'M IMPOSSIBLY romantic, but I think I'm in love with my UPS driver.

The UPS "rank and file," which means the people who do the actual work, voted to accept fifty-five dollars a week until the company agreed to their "demands." Their demands included asking for a raise for part-time workers making eight dollars an hour. The company's original offer was a one-and-a-half-percent increase for full-time workers, none for part-timers. Geez, runaway inflation. Call Alan Greenspan.

You know how Wall Street hates inflation. Not counting executive salaries. For instance, last year Salomon Brothers increased the CEO's salary about one thousand percent to eleven and a half million dollars. *Business Week* says the average compensation for a CEO at a large company increased last year by fifty-four percent, about eighteen times the cost of living and two hundred nine times his average employee's paycheck.

The rich are richer than, well, even the rich. *Newsweek* says in comparable dollars, Bill Gates is about three times as rich as John D. Rockefeller. Warren Buffet has ten times the money Andrew Carnegie did. And my UPS driver — average hourly wage nineteen dollars and ninety-five cents — was the one with nerve enough to say that this is not right. Not fair. Not sane.

Now, I'm not saying I'd like to have the Teamsters running this country. And most of us can name companies crippled by labor demands. But unions, for a generation at least, provided some checks and balance. Lately there has been no balance and not much check.

UPS workers stuck up for a lot of other people. Even people who don't belong to their union. This is a very important moment in the relationship between those who have stock options and those who punch a time clock. A moment long overdue.

OK, maybe it's not love I feel for my driver in brown. Maybe it's just respect. And gratitude. Come back, Bob. It's safe now. I've regained my perspective. Maybe we all have.
— *August, 1997*

CYBER COOKIES AND VIRTUAL GIRLS

I DON'T MEAN to be critical — because I wish them only great success and many merit badges — but when was the last time you bought a Girl Scout cookie from an actual girl?

When I was a Brownie, which is, of course, the Girl Scout farm team, we put on our sashes and peddled our Do-Si-Dos door-to-door. Our parents were not part of the sales force.

This is not to say that our families were not pulled into the cookie net. We hit the streets only after practicing on our grandparents and aunts and uncles. My mom once agreed to be a delivery station, or as they are now called, a cookie cupboard. This is an experience she'd like to repeat about as much as she'd like to be in a high wind without a hairnet.

Samoas and Trefoils were stacked up to the ceiling in the family room along with a shoe box full of money. Nobody was bonded, and we did not have a home security system. We did, however, have a very noisy dog.

By the way, selling Girl Scout cookies is absolutely no

preparation for selling anything else. Everybody buys. For good reason. It's a dependable product at a fair price and has been for sixty years.

A box of Girl Scout cookies only costs two dollars and fifty cents. You get an honest serving, and they taste just like they did back when I was dunking them into milk instead of coffee.

But it is all just too sophisticated these days. The cookie company has a marketing specialist who, first of all, doesn't even call them cookies. She calls them a niche product, and as near as I can figure out, mothers and fathers and aunts and uncles and cousins are the "internal market" and everybody else is the "external market."

My brother was my marketing consultant. He told me that if somebody said they didn't want any cookies, I should cry. And that my optimum sales period was right before dinner and that I should give free samples to the fattest person in the house.

The truth is, most people don't want their little girls out knocking on strange doors.

A Boston troop and one in Hawaii have put their cookies on the Internet and their virtual cookie stores will be taking orders through the end of March.

Myself, I prefer Thin Mints to Cybercookies.

Even if I never see an actual scout.

— *February, 1996*

Eleven

IF THE MEDIUM IS THE MESSAGE, WHAT ARE THEY TRYING TO SAY?

"Yep. I'm gay.
—Ellen DeGeneres

FEELING SICK? DAYTIME TV
CAN CURE YOU

EVERYBODY ALWAYS THINKS they suffer the most when it happens to them, but I can assure you that this misfortune has no regard for race, creed, sex, economic status or your choice of personal hygiene products.

I am speaking, of course, of being trapped with daytime television.

Through no fault of my own, I got the flu. Sneezing and wheezing, I described my symptoms to my doctor in the most florid terms. She told me to quit whining and drink lots of liquids. No drugs. No magic bullet. No leaving the house. My eyes were too swollen for my contact lenses, so I couldn't read.

I guess you know what that means.

Our family doesn't have cable. Or a dish. If God had meant us to have fifty-four channels with continuous reruns of *I Love Lucy*, He would not have invented books. Or conversation. Most of the time we are perfectly happy with our electronic access to news and entertainment.

That's because normally we only use it at night and on weekends when programmers and advertisers believe that people who buy cars and beer and expensive pet-food products will be watching. Networks spend lots of money hiring Cybill Shepherd and Jerry Seinfeld and John Lithgow to entertain these preferred customers.

They love us nighttime people. We have two paychecks, and we're not afraid to use them. However, they have absolutely no respect for people who turn on the television between the hours of nine a.m. and five p.m. In fact, I think it's fair to say that they hate these people and are trying to drive them crazy.

If you don't believe me, then just surround yourself with soggy tissues and a gallon jug of orange juice and a TV remote control and you'll see what I mean.

Charlie Gibson and Katie Couric go their merry way at nine o'clock on the button, leaving us in the hands of Regis and Kathie Lee. Kathie Lee has two children, who will be in therapy for the rest of their lives after they find out what their mother has been telling the nation about their potty training.

Or maybe if they really come unglued, they'll wind up on *Jerry Springer*. Anyone in America who is doing something vile and is willing to talk about it at the top of his lungs can star on Jerry's show. No wonder people are so crazy about Rosie O'Donnell. I watched for three days in a row, and she did not give air time to a single freak. Nor did Oprah.

Of course, another choice is the dreaded TBA, which usually means that it's an infomercial, which is a word invented to avoid coming right out and admitting it's a big sales pitch, uninterrupted by entertainment of any kind.

The one I saw featured a completely baffling demonstration during which a man purposely burned cheese on a nonstick pan, then cleaned it off with a feather duster to wild applause from the audience. I was grateful to return to regular ads from attorneys begging for personal-injury claims.

Kids' shows included Lamb Chop and Charlie Horse fighting over a chair, the insufferable Barnie, Mr. Rogers and something called *Bananas in Pajamas*.

If mornings are dramas recounted by people who look as though Jerry or Geraldo should have run them through a car wash before they show up on the set, afternoon soaps are beautiful people who spend all their time in bed either kissing or in a coma.

Believe me, with all the kissing these people do, they should have lips the size of Volkswagens. And that's basically it until the local teams rescue us at five.

I couldn't wait to get back to work. I'm cured. I think it was the orange juice and the prospect of spending another day with women who are sleeping with their sisters' husbands who are cross-dressing lingerie models. Or watching the bed-bound soap stars. No harm done, except that I worry a little about adults who are stuck at home with this dreck as their reality.

And I worry a lot about the children.

— *September, 1996*

158

JUST NATURALLY GLAMOROUS

MY SISTER-IN-LAW, ELLIE, went to one of those places where they dress you up and fix your hair and makeup before they take your picture. She's so pretty anyway, she just looks like they more or less caught her on a good hair day when she'd had a decent night's rest and hadn't a worry in the world. And while she was thinking of something slightly X-rated.

I don't think it will work for me. To begin with, I don't have a shred of glamour about me that some skillful makeup artist and talented photographer could enhance. The words silk purse and sow's ear spring to mind. Ellie told me they make you show up wearing no makeup and with your hair freshly washed but unstyled. Right. I'll bet I could clear the mall if I strolled through looking like that.

Then, as I understand it, they go to work on you with hot rollers and mousse and hair spray and combs until you look like a country singer. Then they have boxes and bags of cosmetics and spackling compound so they can erase and fill in every real and imagined flaw in your face. They can enlarge skinny lips and slim down fat noses.

I really don't see how it would do much for my self esteem if my husband kept a picture on his desk that everybody either assumed was his girl friend or a glamorous ex-wife he had before he traded down to me. It would almost be worse if people recognized me and just thought I hadn't taken very good care of myself or had been sick.

A friend says she had one done to send to her former husband and his child bride. She doesn't expect ever to see him again but hopes he will think that his memory is faulty or that she started looking better as soon as she wasn't burdened by marriage to him anymore.

Another friend told me her real estate broker had one made for her business cards. Just what everybody wants — a picture of your Realtor in a teddy.

The only benefit I can see would be if you could get the newspapers to agree to use it for your obituary. Laura Pulfer Dead at Ninety-two. "Hmmm," people would say. "She certainly had fat lips and great big hair for an old chick."

— *WVXU radio, May, 1994*

WILL WE LET THE REAL ELLEN INTO OUR LIVES?

WE MADE ELLEN DeGeneres what she is today. So what happens to her next?

Today, she is a thirty-nine-year-old woman looking out from the newsstand, saying, "Yep. I'm gay." Well, she wouldn't have said that if the question hadn't been asked. And the question wouldn't have been asked if we hadn't already known the answer.

Time magazine got the exclusive "confession," but

Newsweek stripped a bright yellow banner over its logo announcing "The outing of Ellen." Not *TV Guide*, not *People* magazine, but the two most important news magazines in the country.

That's because this story has very little to do with television or show business and everything to do with real life.

If *Suddenly Susan's* Brooke Shields, who also has relationship problems on her show, had floated the notion of "discovering" her character's lesbianism, it would have been no big deal. Brooke might even have gotten face time on talk shows that otherwise wouldn't have her on a plate.

Gay and lesbian activists would have stepped forward to kibitz. Provided that Brooke kept the bedroom door closed, the noise would have been modest. Even from the pulpits.

Billy Crystal was an excruciatingly well-adjusted gay man in prime time on *Soap* several years ago. Everybody on the show was squirrelly, except for his character. More important, we all knew that he's married with children "in real life."

Tom Hanks and Antonio Banderas were adorable and acceptable as a gay couple in *Philadephia*. First of all, because the closest they got to a clinch was a slow dance (no dipping, please), and second because Tom Hanks is straight and Mr. Banderas is not only straight but studly.

The uproar isn't just because this is the first mainstream show with a central character who's gay. It's because this is the first show about a lesbian, starring a lesbian. A likable, funny, real person.

How dangerous is that?

Critics will no doubt argue that she is a bad role model for children, as if Ellen will now inspire a generation of lesbians. Much is still to be discovered about sexual orientation, but most experts would agree that seeing a sympathetic portrayal of a gay woman will not turn your fourteen-year-old daughter into a lesbian.

If she's already a lesbian, however, it might keep her from feeling worthless and alone.

Almost nothing about the "coming out" episode of *Ellen* and Ms. DeGeneres's personal revelation was news. It started with a long tease about the sitcom character. The nerdy, hapless Ellen Morgan of television was almost certainly going to be outed this season.

It would have been incredibly cheesy if Ellen DeGeneres had not been by her side. Unnatural, you might say.

Will her show become a weekly visit to a gay bar? Unlikely. Her schtick has always been more Mary Tyler Moore than Sandra Bernhard. Perhaps the point can be firmly and finally made that sexual orientation is simply part of who we are — as is gender, as is race, as is religion. It's important. But it's not everything. Bill Cosby chose to make his comedy more about family than race. And Truman Capote's *In Cold Blood* has never been described as a gay novel.

So, the question has been asked and answered. Ellen Morgan is gay. Ellen DeGeneres is gay. The next question will be answered in places coastal sophisticates sneeringly call "flyover country." Will we now notice that maybe Ellen is not the only one in our lives who is gay? That being gay is more than a movie of the week? We loved Tom and Billy and Antonio. Can we love a real person?

— *April, 1997*

PROTECTING THE WOMENFOLK FROM CYBERPORN

WELL, APPARENTLY IT'S time to adjust our nerd-o-meter. Those of us who have been blissfully computer illiterate, who have made fun of people who can make their IBMs and Macs sing and dance and balance their checkbooks, who have called them computer weenies and made unkind remarks about their pocket protectors must now look at them in a different light.

They are raving sex maniacs.

Newsweek says during a seven-week period, one-point-nine million cyberbrowsers peeked inside the Smithsonian. *Playboy* got four-point-seven million hits in seven days. Now, there's a shock. More Americans are interested in sex than in Grover Cleveland or the history of the buffalo nickel.

The federal government knows what to do about this national scandal. Laws. New laws. Washington will put up with rape, robbery and murder, but they draw the line at dirty pictures.

Co-sponsor of the "decency bill," Sen. Dan Coats said proudly that, among other wonders, this bill will protect women and children. Well, thanks a lot, but we grown-up girls have known how to hit the off switch for quite a while. And when was the last time you heard about somebody getting disgusted to death?

I don't want to appear ungrateful, but I'd say we womenfolk aren't as scared of pictures of great big breasts as we are of real rapists and genuine poverty. We'd rather you give a little more thought to helping us get our kids educated and paying for the groceries. Even Bosnia, for heaven's sake.

Naturally, everybody worries that the nation's children will get a look at this sleaze. And it's true that the average fifth-grader can surf the internet more easily than his parents, but surely the average fifth grader with this kind of equipment has a responsible adult around to just say no.

This seems more reasonable than new laws to restrict not only the fifth graders but the rest of us as well. Newt Gingrich has called the bill headed for the House "a violation of the rights of adults to communicate with each other."

As for us poor, helpless women, let our computers alone. We can slam the doors of the chat rooms ourselves.

— *National Public Radio,*
July, 1995

HOW SINCERE ARE CELEBRITIES PAID TO BE?

DID YOU FEEL sorry for Kathie Lee Gifford when it was discovered that she'd sold her name to an outfit that makes money on the backs of children? She said she didn't know, and I believe her. Should she have been held accountable anyway?

Holding stars responsible for the products they hawk could have a chilling effect on celebrity endorsements. Soon, we may have to make our buying decisions without assistance from noted consumerists such as Ed McMahon and Bill Cosby and Whoopie Goldberg.

There must be some reason marketers think we'll buy anything from famous persons. Why else would they put June Allyson in diapers and ambush us in primetime with Charles Barkley's deodorant? Why else would they think we care whether George Foreman is "not going to pay a lot for this muffler"?

I wonder how they decide a particular celebrity would make a compelling case for their product. It's easy to see why Nike would go after Michael Jordan. We think he might actually know something about athletic shoes. But I always wondered why Pepsi thought we'd make a soft drink selection based on Michael Jackson's recommendation. Weren't they afraid that the American public thinks he's so profoundly bent that we wouldn't risk using his plastic surgeon, his hair-dresser or his cola?

Somehow they must have gotten the impression that we'll pay more attention to advice from big names. I wonder how they got that idea.

Perhaps they noticed that the Congress of the United States consults Robert Redford on environmental matters and Meryl Streep on pesticides. (I don't remember what Meryl had to say about Alar and apples, but I'll bet she said it with a fabulous accent.)

Thank goodness Congress stopped short of a special sub-committee to study Barbra Streisand's insights into foreign policy or Hugh Grant's research into the plight of working women.

But it didn't take long for Kathie Lee, formerly the com-pletely astonished accomplice in the exploitation of children, to co-star at a press conference with the U.S. Secretary of Labor and later to testify before Congress about child labor in the rag trade.

So, how gullible are we anyway? Surely we know that Rosie O'Donnell and Penny Marshall didn't really just run into each other in the aisles at K-Mart. Still, famous personalities are different from actors who merely read a script gushing about gum and beer and motor oil. Even though we probably know better, it sounds like a personal recommendation to us. More believable. That's why they get the big bucks.

Just how much guilt does Kathie Lee share with the sweat-shops that produce her clothing line? Should she have been expected to know anything about the company that makes the blouses she sells?

It's just a job. They don't really owe us anything. They're just paid to say they like all this stuff. Should Kathie Lee have made it her business to know anything about the company? Should Candice? Should Whoopie? Should Michael?

It depends on how much their name is worth to them.

— *June, 1996*

ADVENTURES IN THE LAND OF CHAT TV

NOT LONG AGO, I had a root canal and I hosted a television talk show. The root canal was less painful. Of course, I was fully medicated for my tooth, and all they gave me for the talk show was coffee, Diet Coke and a doughnut.

Dick Von Hoene, the regular host of TKR Cable's *Northern Kentucky Magazine,* had an emergency involving a cart, a bag and a nine-iron. Dick said I would be the perfect sub, and, from his point of view, I was. When he negotiates a new contract, I'm sure he will play a tape of my performance for his boss.

"Just be natural," the show's producer told me. Ha. If it's all so natural, then why does it take Oprah two hours to get ready? Why does Tom Brokaw wear makeup? Not wishing to look like a poor print cousin, I laid on the hair gel and eye liner.

I looked like Little Richard.

When I arrived at the station, I learned that a guest had bailed out. "We'll get somebody else," I was told. "Or you can improvise." It is now twenty minutes to air time. This show is live.

I had no idea that flop sweat could begin before the actual flop.

The cameraman taught me signals they'd be using to make sure that I didn't blab during their commercials. They start warning you at three minutes, then the signals get increasingly ominous until the fifteen-second warning, which is a raised fist.

I do not know whether this is the signal for everybody. Or just me.

My way of dealing smoothly with the end of a segment was to look nervous at three minutes, then become increasingly agitated. At the one-minute signal, I would usually ask my guest a question that could not possibly be answered in less than ten minutes.

When the floor director — who surely must have an ulcer the size of a basketball — gave me the raised fist, my technique was to freeze, then clap a hand over my guest's mouth and shriek, "We'll be right back. Probably."

They gave me great guests. There was a social worker who kept patting my hand and telling me I was doing "just fine." But I'm pretty sure I caught her rolling her eyes when I forgot the name of the show, the name of her agency, her name. And mine.

Lucille Treganowan, "American's most trusted auto mechanic," was next. *The New York Times* calls her an "unflappable, khaki-clad grandmother who also happens to be an award-winning automotive expert." I think I saw her flap a little when I told her that I have no idea where the transmission fluid is located on my car, which I regard as a purse on wheels.

She wrote *Lucille's Car Care*, which Lucille says will save me money, plus win respect from my mechanic. I wonder whether, instead of respect, he would give me a loaner. Lucille was also on David Letterman's show. My impression is that she wishes she was back with Dave, even if he did get her to admit on national TV that she has a lead foot.

Last was Dr. Michael Palmer, who writes medical thrillers. He says Larry King wouldn't let him plug his book. So, just to show him that my heart is in the right place, I mention it every chance I get. I am hoping he will remember how accommodating I was if I ever need a complimentary tonsillectomy.

Then, there are just a few minutes to fill. So I fill them with nervous laughter. I am getting a thumbs up from the director and the producer. This is going very well, I think. Then everyone in the studio is jabbing their thumbs in the air. And making faces.

It seems that is the signal to "throw it" to news. I finally throw it, and everybody collapses.

You were not inept, the producer says.

But I was not ept.

"Really, we'd love to have you back sometime."

OK, but next time I think we should all be fully medicated.

— *June, 1996*

Twelve

CHAPTERS FROM THE
NOSEBLEED FILES

---

*"When your brain clicks,
you just do it."*
—Justin Evegam

Sometimes No News Is
The Best News

KATHY SCHAFER OF Springdale called to report a nosebleed.

I guess she didn't realize that a newsworthy incident would be more like forty nosebleeds as the result of unarmed gang violence. Or maybe one nosebleed if it happened to, say, Elizabeth Dole. Or Socks the Cat. Or Brad Pitt.

Well, it was just one nose, and it belonged to Kathy's husband, Don, who is retired from a very responsible job at a very important Cincinnati company. But just keeping your head down and working hard for thirty or forty years won't make you famous. So that's probably why Kathy called me instead of Deborah Norville or Mary Hart.

Kathy and Don had two of their four grandchildren for the day. Now, again, this is simply not news. They were not abusing these children. And the children were not fugitives from justice. Nobody is estranged from anybody else. They like each other and get together every holiday to exchange gifts or eat too much. Sometimes both. That's probably why she called me instead of Jerry Springer.

The Schafers drove out to Sharon Woods, seven hundred fifty-five acres with big old trees and picnic benches and a thirty-five-acre fishing lake. Everybody can use the facilities if they behave. You are not interviewed by a membership committee to assess your suitability before you are issued a parking sticker.

Stickers cost three dollars and get you into any county park, including this one, which is particularly nice. There are ramps and broad paths and plenty of ways to get around, even if you have a few extra impediments. Kathy, who has multiple sclerosis, is in a wheelchair, and Don walks with a cane.

The cane is temporary — recent surgery — and she is used to the chair. Diagnosed with MS forty years ago, she has had the chair for ten. No big deal, according to Kathy. They live in an apartment building, where the manager built a ramp so Kathy can just zip right out the door to her car. There are steps down to the mailbox, but her mail is delivered right to the door.

Well, this really is just about the most useless piece of information I've gotten yet. Her mailman apparently has not murdered any of his co-workers, plus he walks up seven steps every day, even though I am sure that his civil-service manual does not require him to do so.

His name is Mark, and just because he works a little harder than he has to, he definitely is not newsworthy either. Nor is the woman from the Shafers' church, who brings Communion to Kathy every Sunday.

By now, a few minutes have passed, and I am surprised that I have not hung up the telephone to go on to more worthy and uplifting stories, such as crack babies or the latest pilgrimage to Dr. Jack Kervorkian.

I must be losing my touch.

Anyway, Kathy said they were just getting ready to throw their fishing lines in the water when Don's nose suddenly began to bleed. Another grandfather, on an outing with his ten grandchildren, ran back to his ice chest. He put a cold pack on Don's neck. A couple more people helped him to a bench.

No one's pocket was picked. No one's purse was snatched.

There were more volunteer tissues than you could count. Somebody even donated a real handkerchief.

One of the bystanders called the park paramedics. Probably an overreaction. By the time they arrived, the bleeding had almost stopped. Everything was okay, and Don was a little embarrassed by the commotion. In all, about a dozen people came to the aid of this one ordinary nosebleed.

Kathy wishes she could thank them all, but she didn't get anybody's name. I guess she hasn't heard about the very prudent practice of taking names at events such as these in case you later think of a way you could sue somebody.

"I wouldn't have called you," she says apologetically, "except it's just one of those things that reminds you how nice people can be. It sort of restores your faith in human nature." Well, yes it does. And so do you.

Stop the presses.

— *August, 1996*

FERGIE IS OFFICIALLY American. I suspected it all along.

When the Duchess of York, Sarah Ferguson, came to this country a few months ago, I noticed that she didn't have any dogs with her. She didn't ask where we kept the horses. She cheerfully answered personal questions. She giggled. I heard rumors that she was drinking coffee instead of tea.

She was funny and open and, sometimes, a little silly. Completely lovable, if you ask me.

And now, she is the new spokeswoman for that most American institution, Weight Watchers. Can you see any other member of the Royal Family getting weighed in public or discussing the benefits of the Fat and Fiber Plan?

The duchess is supposed to attend Weight Watchers meetings all over the country. Do you suppose anybody will really want to know what she had for breakfast? Or will they be asking more important questions, such as: Doesn't Princess Anne get on your last nerve?

Or, did you ever get a chance to see what the Queen carries in her purse? A Sam's card? Dog treats? A bungee cord?

The initial news from Weight Watchers is that Fergie's weight is none of our beeswax. They said she's in the one hundred thirty-one to one hundred fifty-eight-pound range, which is where she ought to be for her height of five feet, seven and a half inches. She's supposed to be paid a million dollars and lose five more pounds.

What's next? I think we all know, if I'm right about this American thing. Soon there will be little Fergie YoYo Diet Dolls. She will be making an appearance on the shopping channel hawking cubic zirconium tiaras.

After one season with Weight Watchers, she'll declare herself a free agent and sign a multi-year contract with Jenny Craig.

— WVXU radio, April, 1997

GUILTY OF
AGGRAVATED KINDNESS

SYLVIA STAYTON IS guilty as sin. She's the sixty-two-year-old Cincinnati woman arrested for putting coins in meters by cars owned by strangers. Her diabolical plan was to save them parking tickets.

She appears to be guilty as sin. Let's convict her of aggravated kindness. And this is not her first offense. Active in her church, she has fed expired parking meters for years and also has been known to give money to charity. While waiting to be released from jail, she led other prisoners in prayer.

Thank goodness, for a few hours at least, the streets of Cincinnati were safe from this woman.

And somehow the fact that she is a grandmother has become tacit proof of her innocence and worth. Being a grandmother myself, I do not immediately picture a little old lady with her hair in a bun, wearing an apron and a dab of vanilla behind her ears. I picture me. And I am painfully aware that I do not bake cookies or lead a blameless life. I am not wise. Sometimes I have a big mouth.

City law forbids "re-metering" or putting more coins in a meter after a car has been parked for the maximum allowable time. This is to protect merchants who would like to attract customers with cars but who do not like the idea of paying for a parking lot. So the streets become part of their business plan. And the police become their unofficial employees.

Curiously, Mrs. Stayton was not charged with this crime. She was charged with obstructing official business after she put a coin in the meter of a car being ticketed by a police officer. The question, of course, would be whose business? Which official?

The police officer says he told her it is against the law to plug expired parking meters. He says she began to debate. Loudly. She says the only time she raised her voice was to scream when he yanked on her arm.

I have seen police defuse violent situations with great skill. They're trained to do that. I assume they will not use their power to bluster or bully or deliver harmless people to our clogged courtrooms. I also assume anybody who has been around long enough to be a grandmother knows it's not wise to argue with a police officer.

But police officers who are supposed to protect us from

rapists and murderers have better things to do than throw the book at citizens who flout obscure and witless laws.

Maybe Mrs. Stayton acted unwisely. Maybe both parties overreacted. Of course, she was only packing a coin purse. And the police officer carries a gun.

— *October, 1996*

THE '90S NEUROSIS OF CHOICE

WHAT THIS WORLD needs is more compulsive personalities. And if you don't believe me, you haven't seen what one can do to an untidy room. Or an understaffed office.

I discussed this theory with someone who not only has studied psychology but runs once a week with a behavioral therapist. They have been doing this long enough to be able to run ten miles and talk at the same time. I find it astonishing that women this intelligent think it's a good idea to suck in great lungfuls of urban air while pounding their knees into pabulum and dislodging important internal parts.

How healthy will you be, I ask her, when your uterus falls out and you trip over it and break your neck? I hope it will not erode your confidence in them to know that they also think it is a good idea to run five miles then eat two dips of chocolate chip ice cream each. This will be recommended by the American Heart Association right after fried cheese as a bedtime snack. But I digress.

My two experts, whom I will call Jan and Linda because those are their names and it will give them a tiny thrill to hear me flirting with their professional ruination by almost identifying them, have explained true compulsive behavior to me. It sounds pretty useful.

They're people who will come to work on time and never leave dirty dishes in the sink at the company lunchroom. They also would never leave mysterious containers in the communal refrigerator long enough that it becomes a petri dish. They will never walk off with your ballpoint pen because they're afraid you may have put it in your mouth.

They will never steal the *People* magazine from their doctor's office. In fact, they will never read used magazines because they would not like to think they're reading something that somebody else might have sneezed on.

I think they sound wonderful. In fact, I want my company to hire more of them. I think I'll ask the personnel department. When you send in your resume, under qualifications, just put "anal retentive."

I promise we'll know exactly what you mean.

— *WVXU radio,*
September, 1993

THIS LITTLE STORY
IS A BIG DEAL

HEY, LOOK WHAT I found. Good news. At the ballpark. Yes, our ballpark. Better than that, this is a story about the Cincinnati Reds and Opening Day that will not humiliate or defame anybody. Hard to believe, I know.

Furthermore, it's not about winning or losing. It is not provocative or controversial. It won't get anybody in hot water or on *Nightline* or on the cover of *Sports Illustrated.* Jay Leno won't find anything here for his opening monologue.

It's even — get this — a story about children who are neither troubled nor troublemakers.

The tale starts with a little boy named Christopher Harris, a third grader and Reds fan who was struggling with cursive while Eric Davis was batting on April first. When Christopher, a wiry kid with dishwater blond hair in a skater cut, got home from school, he watched television clips of the game he had missed that day.

He saw replays of umpire John McSherry collapsing at home plate in front of five thousand Opening Day fans. He saw the fifty-one-year-old man try to stagger off the field. Then he saw some Cincinnati fans boo when the game was canceled.

"He was sad — and embarrassed," says his mother, Vickie Harris. "He said he wanted to think of something to make the man's family feel better and let them know that not everybody in Cincinnati felt that way."

Didn't we all.

The boy talked his mom out of some construction paper and hauled it off to school. His class produced twenty-three hand-lettered cards from the heart. The artwork was original. The sentiments, more or less along the lines of, "I hope you feel better."

In the midst of a swarm of people who were worried about how they felt about this man's death, these kids got it right, and they figured it out without any help from Hallmark or their parents. Or, certainly, from anything they were seeing in the news.

Christopher's mother bundled up the cards and sent them off to the Reds office, asking that the cards be forwarded to "John McSherry's loved ones."

The cards went to the veteran umpire's longtime companion, Marion Doyle, and her son and daughter, who lived with John McSherry in Dobbs Ferry, N.Y. Ms. Doyle said the package arrived on "a very tough day" and that she was "touched and uplifted by their innocent thoughtfulness."

So when Marion Doyle got a manila envelope filled with cards from a bunch of nine-year-olds who seemed to understand what really happened at Riverfront Stadium on April first, nineteen ninety-six, she answered back. She sent thirty Reds home-game tickets to Christopher's class, enough for all the kids plus their chauffeur/moms.

Big deal. So, it's just a baseball game, a bunch of kids, a nice woman. There are plenty of worse reasons to celebrate.

— April, 1996

WILL THE NEW GOOD BOYS GET THEIR DAY?

PLEASE UNDERSTAND THAT I already know this isn't fair, but I'm going to do it anyway.

A little over a week ago, two teen-agers found ten thousand dollars in a trash bin and did not steal it. This extraordinary event made its way to the front page of *The Enquirer*, at least three radio stations and, eventually, onto national television. No less than *Good Morning, America's* Joan Lunden interviewed Matt Disher, fourteen, and Kris Miller, fifteen.

In case you were in Aruba or an *ESPN* trance at the time, here's what happened. Matt pitched his Spree candy wrapper toward a trash bin next to an ATM machine. It missed, and when he bent down to retrieve it and try again, he saw bundles of cash. Now, right away I love the idea that he was persistent about using the trash bin.

Next, the boys checked to see if it was real. Then they replaced the money and called the police five hours later. During that time, they said they talked about a drum set that Matt wants and some car speakers Kris covets.

I think it was probably like the period of time between when I buy my lottery ticket and when someone else wins.

Eventually, they turned in the money.

They are not heroes. They are nice boys who did the right thing — after, it would appear to me, wrestling with their conscience, a drum set and some car speakers. Hey, I'm not making any judgments. I fear that I might still be wrestling. And losing.

About a week later, two other boys, exactly the same ages as Matt and Kris, chased a robbery suspect and held him until the police arrived.

Justin Evegan, fourteen, and Donte Ulmer, fifteen, both of Walnut Hills, had missed their downtown bus to school when a man grabbed a woman's purse. The woman, Carolyn Johnson, was in a wheelchair outside the John Weld Peck Federal Building when a man grabbed her wallet from the purse around her neck.

Then "he just ran smack in front of us," Justin said. "Me and Donte heard the lady saying, 'Get him, get him,' and we just jumped up and took off after him."

That's my favorite part. It was instinctive. They didn't have time to think it over. On top of that, when they caught the guy, he threw some of the money at the boys. "He was like, 'Here, take some of the money and let me go,'" Justin said.

No dice.

They held him until police arrived. "When your brain clicks, you just do it," Justin said.

Maybe it is what we do without thinking that is truly heroic. I've never been tested, but I've always hoped that I would automatically do the brave and honorable thing.

So, as I said, it's really not fair to compare the two incidents, assigning a greater value to reflex. Maybe it's simply good news and better news. I'm not sorry that the first two kids got so much attention.

But, Donte and Justin, I hope you get your fifteen minutes of fame and more. I hope your family and friends and radio and television fawn all over you. And I have only one more thing to say: I want to be just like you when I grow up.

— *March, 1996*

Thirteen

WINNING THE
HUMAN RACE

"We're tired of all the bad news."
—Survey response

SOMEBODY SAID ONCE that journalists are just reporters with better haircuts. And heaven knows that whatever we're calling ourselves these days, we're about as popular as lawyers and people who sell Amway products. Every time our newspaper does a survey of its readers, they tell us the same thing: "We're tired of all the bad news."

Our answer is always that we cannot help it if the news is bad. We don't make the news. We just tell you about the news there is. So, get off our backs. (Actually, the people in charge won't let us say the last part, but that's what we're thinking.)

Nobody has ever complained, as far as I know, about the dozens of stories we've printed about one Victoria Koch, age fourteen, owner of a purple bicycle, aspiring ballet dancer, saxophone player and thoroughly positive person.

For those of us who report the news, Victoria's story began in February, nineteen ninety-three, when she underwent a double lung transplant, radical treatment for cystic fibrosis. We identified her as a Warren County girl, the daughter of William and Pamela. Over the years, they became Tory and Bill and Pam. Sometimes we were letting our readers know of some fund-raiser or another. Good news, sort of.

Once we had a story about a cameo role she played in a Cincinnati Ballet production of Cinderella. She signed autographs afterward. But most of the stories were about some new battle for this child. Most of them were scary as hell. Most of them were life and death.

None of them was bad news, at least according to one who would know.

"Most of the bad news is violence," Tory said. "When you hear about a little girl who needed a double lung transplant and got it, it's just good news." This from a kid who probably never took an unimpeded breath in her life.

"I wake up, do the day, go to sleep, wake up, have fun. I don't think of death at all. Everybody has their time to go." Is this kid for real? Well, yes she is, and so is her family.

Over the years and more than a hundred trips to Pittsburgh Children's Hospital for everything from chicken pox to tissue rejection to mystery viruses, every discouraging word about Tory Koch's battle to stay alive came from somebody outside her family.

For instance, Bill Koch said Monday, "This is kinda neat, you know. We get to see God at work." The thing is, they have faith. They continually invoke the G word. And if there is anything that makes us more uncomfortable than good news, it is somebody who talks about religion.

Remember when Scott O'Grady was rescued from his downed plane in Bosnia? In almost every interview, he said something about how important his faith was to his survival. Everybody from Joan Lunden to Bryant Gumbel just sailed right by that one.

If he'd said he was sure that his daily twenty-minute aerobic workout was important to his survival, they would have been interviewing people at his gym. But he mentioned prayer and everybody just squirmed and went on to ask him about how many bugs he ate or how he managed to suck on his socks for water.

Something about this family has let them be in the spotlight for two-and-a-half years, and they just seem to get better, more likeable. The kids should be brats by now. Tory has a twin sister, and there are three other kids, ages five, nine and eleven. They are polite and well-behaved and, well, good.

"Two-and-a-half years ago, Victoria was nearly dead," says her father. "We've had two-and-a-half of the best years. We've gotten to do everything we wanted to do."

I will never write about Tory Koch's death, but I am privileged to write about her life. And in the midst of ventilators and steroids and needles, that was always the good news.

— *October, 1995*

IS IT TOO LATE FOR THE REST OF US TO JOIN THE CLUB?

THE BOOKS WERE just an excuse. But it was a good one, and they used it for sixty-five years.

The Pro and Con Book Club started informally, as these

things sometimes do. Elizabeth Greene fell ill just after graduation from high school. "Tuberculosis, I think it was," says Edith Biery Seale.

Mrs. Seale was one of many schoolmates who went to visit her stricken friend. The young girls took books. And they talked. Elizabeth's mother, Joy Greene, told them they were a book club, gave them a name and a regular meeting date.

"She was a lovely woman, Mrs. Greene." This information comes from Aimie Greene, a daughter-in-law, so I think we can depend on it as truth. And it appears that this lovely woman figured out a way to keep these school girls gathered around her housebound daughter with the subtle nudge of a monthly meeting date. Furthermore, she engineered a plan that elevated the visits from dutiful sickroom house calls to lively literary discussions. Her daughter was a member, not an invalid.

A mother's master stroke.

When Elizabeth died in nineteen thirty-four, the club continued. By then, there were about a dozen members, including another Greene daughter-in-law, Ettamae Waggal. "After the book report, we'd talk about everything else — boyfriends, husbands and anybody who wasn't there."

She says with four kids to chase she "had no business being in a book club." Sometimes she didn't have time to read the book. "But, of course, I went anyway and confessed." Of course she did.

By now this book club is beginning to sound familiar.

Some of them were card clubs, where women pretended to play bridge while they gave each other advice on children with croup and husbands with cholesterol. Others were garden clubs, where they planted apple trees and beautiful boulevards while exchanging maternity clothes and recipes.

Their lives revolved around their families and their homes, but "club" was a regular respite from pabulum and furniture polish. During the war years, they counted ration stamps for luncheons and desserts. But they continued to meet. And talk. And listen.

There have been hundreds of books read, dozens of children reared, decades of weddings and funerals and graduations. As they grew older and eyesight dimmed, they went from evening meetings to daytime, from once a month to once in a while to hardly ever.

They laugh. They nudge each other. They roll their eyes and use the exquisite conversational shorthand earned by years of history. They remind each other of the past, sometimes interrupting gently to correct a name, clarify a relationship. One in a wheelchair. One whose hands tremble. One who loses, occasionally, the thread of conversation.

They are, quite simply, old friends. And I can't help feeling a twinge of envy, wondering if women in my generation and the next — who are getting child rearing tips from the au pair and recipes from Martha Stewart — will ever know how it feels to be one of these women.

Their discussion is lively and intimate and funny and dear. But it is not literary, at least while I am listening. So, I don't know if they really love books. But I know that they love each other.

— July, 1997

THE DELUXE SPORTS PACKAGE

I WAS THINKING about Dennis Rodman, which I hardly ever do. But each time I turn on the television, I have another chance to see him kick the photographer in what has delicately been referred to as the groin area.

I couldn't help comparing him to Andy Dragan, fourteen, my teammate at a Special Olympics competition.

Mr. Rodman is a professional athlete. This means he is paid buckets of money, has expensive shoes named after him and is as bad as he wants to be. He has more than ten thousand career rebounds for his Chicago Bulls. This must be why they still want him on their team after he assaulted someone in public. In the groin area.

Myself, I felt lucky to be on Ellen Schauer and Andy Dragan's team, as what this organization generously calls "celebrity captain." Ellen, fourteen, is blond, scrappy and outgoing. She never gave up on me, even when I was zero for three in the softball pitch. She spit on the ball for good luck, and although that experience was a little juicier than I expected, it worked. I made the next toss through the strike zone.

Andy showed me how to hold the putter. When I sent the golf ball careening off the shoes of a very nice woman, who was nowhere near the artificial green, Andy told me I'd probably do better at bowling.

I didn't.

On top of that, I gave him an encouraging pat on the shoulder just as he was releasing a basketball from the free-throw line, surely causing him to miss. Kicking anybody, even me, was the furthest thing from his mind. He was giving pointers to another kid. On the other team.

This is not unusual. Special Olympics, competition for children and adults with mental and development disabilities, is always a wonderful surprise package of good sports. Two years ago, a couple of runners from the same school trained together for the hundred-meter sprint. As they neared the tape, one slowed and reached for the other. They grinned and crossed the finish line, hand-in-hand.

Last year, a team was being badly beaten in the state co-ed basketball tournament. With fifteen seconds left, the score was forty-five to ten. A five-foot, two-inch guard chased her five-foot, nine-inch opponent as though the game had just begun. The taller kid looked up at the clock and saw three seconds. His little guard still had her hands in the air, defending the basket. He passed her the ball. She dribbled down the court and made a lay-up shot.

The crowd roared.

Now, I do not want to give you the impression that there are not some fine athletes among the Special Olympics participants. They work hard, and they will spend countless hours training. This is an experience that is important to them, and I'm sure they enjoy winning.

But not at any cost.

Their oath is, "Let me win. But if I cannot win, let me be brave in the attempt."

I like that. And I believe that I was very brave when I threw basketballs that didn't hit the net, the rim or the backboard. And I think I behaved myself when my bowling ball missed the head pin. But then, I had exceptional role models.

And I know that it's not fair, really, to compare Dennis Rodman to Andy Dragan.

Mr. Rodman is clearly outclassed.

— *January, 1997*

WHAT'S THE GOING RATE FOR A GOOD MOM?

AND NOW, "THE mom thing" becomes a political bomb. This has already been a neighborhood bomb, pitting working mothers against women who choose to be full-time moms. "Do you work outside the home?" we have learned to ask.

This lesson was lost on Hamilton County Recorder Eve Bolton. Challenger Rebecca Prem Groppe, she says, is just a stay-at-home mother. "Surely, she doesn't think being a mom is a job," Ms. Bolton said. "That's supposed to be a love thing."

Well, of course it is a love thing, and it's a hard-work thing, if I may say so. Anybody — male or female — who has been at home with a child knows that you return to the office to rest up.

Maybe the problem is that it's hard to put a price tag on "the mom thing." Wouldn't you just know that help fell right out of the mailbox and into my lap? A letter from the Professional Domestic Institute promises training for "household managers — butlers and personal assistants, serving today's families."

The Columbus firm offers eight courses of study. Tuition is twelve hundred dollars per course or forty-eight hundred dollars for the whole shebang — or, as it is known about the institute, the Professional Management Course. For instance, you can start out with the household manager/butler class, including personal standards, family psychology, correspondence, record keeping and household inventory.

More advanced courses teach menu planning, special dietary needs, low-fat cooking, kitchen organization and selecting quality foods. In other words, grocery shopping for finicky kids and a husband who is trying to drop fifteen pounds before his high school reunion.

Well, here is the good part. The course materials also included a section on what graduates might expect in their pay envelopes. There's a careful warning that the quoted salaries do not include benefits or bonuses, which will come as a surprise to exactly zero stay-at-home moms.

Pardon me if I sound a little biased, but I've never had a job I thought was as demanding as being a mother and housekeeper. And, by the way, this is a job that often is done in the evenings when a woman comes home from a lesser job as, say, vice president of a bank or chief financial officer of a big company or TV anchor.

Anyway, I just looked at the jobs that seemed to apply to the moms I know: baby sitter, nanny, house cleaner, maid, cook, household manager. I ignored the jobs like major domo, who apparently has servants to do the scut work, only providing "continuity of staff, service and coordination between all properties."

I concentrated on basics, such as "responsible for the family's meals, cleanup and organization of the kitchen, procurement of equipment, supplies and food." The institute suggests this particular service is worth twenty-four thousand dollars to sixty thousand dollars a year. Minimum charge for the total package is one hundred fifty-three thousand, six hundred sixty dollars. It costs four hundred thirty-eight thousand, seven hundred twenty dollars for the deluxe.

So, it appears to me that "the mom thing" is really not so very different from "the work thing."

Except for the love, of course.

— *September, 1996*

LIVING THE ZOO LIFE

I LOVE ZOOS. In fact, I'm thinking of living in one.

A precedent has been set. Henrik Lehmann and Malene Botoft moved into the Copenhagen Zoo right next to the baboons and monkeys. Fully clothed, surrounded by Plexiglas, they are on display — eating, scratching and fighting over the television remote control.

Henrik said they don't notice visitors any longer. "If I want to pick my nose or my toes, now I do it." When he wants to relax from the rigors of grooming, he can use the computer, books, stereo or television. Meanwhile Malene is probably racking up a big tab on the Psychic Hotline.

They are supposedly part of an experiment to remind visitors of the ties between humans and nature. I suspect Henrik and Malene just found a cushy place to hang out and pick their toes while their kitchen is being remodeled.

Zoos are not big cages anymore. They're devoted to the comfort of their creatures. Zoo officials have said they tried to make the environment as realistic as possible. Geez, if I get somebody to agree to take me in, I hope they know that they'll have to get their staff to round up dust balls for underneath my bed. And popcorn for under the sofa cushions.

Most modern zoos also devote themselves to the survival of the world's plants and animals. If they could educate the homo sapiens of the world their job would be ninety-five percent done. We are the ones, of course, who endanger the endangered species.

So, I'd like to help Henrik and Malene encourage people to think about their ties to nature. In fact, I'd like to help people resist ruining nature. And have more respect for the critters in the other cages.

Otherwise, we'll all have to find someplace else to live.

— *September, 1996*

FAMILY VALUE

IT HAS BEEN said that you can tell a lot about people from their families. My experience is that your family tells a lot about you. Literally.

For instance, recently I missed a family wedding because I was sunning myself on a beach. My brother, Steven, told everyone that I couldn't be there because I was at the Betty Ford Clinic. Well, not everybody. He told my eighty-year old uncle that I was in jail. He also tells people that the first words out of my mouth when I was a baby were "Steven did it."

My brother is completely adorable and has a great sense of humor and everybody knows we are crazy about each other and he's just kidding. Probably.

Of much greater concern is my mother. She tells everyone that I'm beautiful and accomplished and intelligent. As you can imagine, it is a terrible shock for her friends when they meet me. So, you can't believe everything you hear about me from my mom, but the fact that she honestly believes her children are wonderful probably tells you a lot about how terrific it was growing up as her kid.

Most everybody knows there are some true and useful things to be learned from a person's family. A lot of people who don't like Bill and Hillary Clinton will certainly concede that they've done a fine job with their daughter. Who knows? It might even win him a vote or two.

Our home life, of course, stays with us long after we leave home. When I have just done something amazingly stupid, I always recover my equilibrium by remembering how smart my mother thinks I am. And, just the other day, when I was stopped for speeding on Columbia Parkway, I had an almost irresistible urge to look the cop right in the eye and say, "Steven did it."

— *WVXU, April, 1994*

THE GOLDEN BOY

BILL CLINTON IS the luckiest man in America. He went back to his thirty-third high school reunion as President of the United States and leader of the free world. Most of us would be satisfied if we could just go back in more or less the same weight division. With more or less our original teeth.

Mr. Clinton returned to his old high school in a limousine, not a minivan or a station wagon. He reported to the stage tanned, buffed up and with a full head of hair. His kid is in a good school, and his wife still fits into her wedding dress. He has his finger on the button and could turn us all — including the playground bully — into charcoal briquettes if he chose. He has been seen in the company of Barbra Streisand and Tiger Woods.

Does it get any better than this?

The Associated Press described him as "the golden boy who led the band." A half dozen cheerleaders from the class of nineteen sixty-four, attired in flared skirts and saddle shoes, stormed the stage and hugged Mr. Clinton.

Now, I don't know how it was in Hot Springs, Arkansas, thirty-three years ago, but where I went to school, the cheerleaders wouldn't storm the stage for anybody less than the quarterback of the football team.

The future commander in chief was remembered as the student who often was let out of classes to speak to the Optimists or the Elks about his White House meeting with John F. Kennedy, which consisted of about a two-second handshake and a photo op. He was with a bunch of Boys Nation delegates, at the head of the pack by dint of long legs and perhaps the first recorded instance of dork walking.

Biographer David Maraniss says Mr. Clinton, who graduated fourth in a class of three hundred sixty-three, was regarded by teachers as a model youth. Again, I don't know how things worked in Hot Springs, but if teachers at our high school went around saying that one of the boys was a "model youth," that was good for a public de-pantsing.

Or a wedgie, at the very least.

Instead, Mr. Clinton's classmates want to name the school after him. The President was the headliner for a reunion of all graduates of Hot Springs High School, which closed its doors in nineteen ninety. Now, the city wants to turn the eighty-three-year-old, red-brick school into the William Jefferson Clinton Cultural Campus, a commercial arts center and Clinton museum.

Mr. Clinton told his classmates modestly that he didn't think he was old enough for the honor. "But if it helps raise another nickel, I accept and I thank you. I'm profoundly honored."

As well he might be.

For those of us who join him at the head of the line of Baby Boomers, he was the signal that, finally, we were in charge. He took over for a man who fought in World War II, just like our fathers. He had doubts about the Vietnam War, just like us. He tried to smoke dope, and he listened to our music. His wife worked "outside the home."

We all have selective memories of ourselves in high school. It's probably the only thing that saves us from a life on Prozac. And class reunions are the ideal place to succeed, to update history, if not rewrite it. The nerd is a computer millionaire. The ugly duckling is a swan.

We'd be proud if the class of nineteen sixty-four's "golden boy" is remembered for more than Whitewater or Monica Lewinski or John Huang or a seven-seat, thirty-one-jet hot tub on the South Lawn of the White House. But history books have tougher standards than yearbooks.

— *October, 1997*

Fourteen

SMALL, UNFORGIVABLE

LOSSES

"Where is your baby?"
—Nosy Villager

WHO CHARTED THIS FLIGHT PLAN?

WHEN A SEVEN-YEAR-OLD "pilot" was killed, one of the first questions asked was whether we should change the federal aviation regulations. That's sort of like putting up a sign prohibiting roller-skating on interstate highways. There are some things we big people ought to know instinctively.

The really hard questions should be put to adults who made it all possible. We should be grilling them instead of the Federal Aviation Administration. Some of us already think there are plenty of laws — more than enough, really — governing our lives. What about this child's parents? Where were they?

Jessica Dubroff's father was right behind her, literally, and her mother, figuratively. A neighbor wept, talking to reporters about her "charisma" and saying she was "seven years old going on twenty."

Nonsense.

She had to be strapped into a booster seat so she could see out the Cessna's windows. Somebody built aluminum extensions so this child, who was just a little more than four feet tall, could reach the rudder pedals. Somebody gave her a baseball cap that said "Women fly."

She was a little girl.

Cheyenne, Wyoming, was buffeted by wind and driving sleet during takeoff that morning. Jessica flew the day before on two hours of sleep. Her flight instructor, also killed in the crash, was next to her, but the child definitely was at the controls during takeoff.

"Clearly, I would want all my children to die in a state of joy," Lisa Blair Hathaway, Jessica's mother, said right after her daughter and former husband crashed. "What more could I ask for? I would prefer it was not at age seven, but, God, she went with her joy and her passion, and her life was in her hands."

Well, that would be the point, wouldn't it?

There's a reason every child is issued parents at birth instead of a Visa card, a job application and the key to an apartment. They need guidance. They need advice. They need help. They need to have somebody to keep their little fingers out of light sockets.

I'm sorry to speak unkindly of the dead, but when I saw file film of Jessica's father I saw every soccer daddy who ever stood along the sidelines on a Saturday afternoon screaming at his five-year-old.

I know you've seen them, too, especially when the kids are little. Especially when they're little girls. I can remember when my daughter, Meg, started playing soccer. She was about five, I think. My husband and I showed up faithfully with orange slices and soda when it was our turn. We helped buy uniforms and cheered from the sidelines.

But we never understood what all the screaming was about. It wasn't the kids. The little girls in the back were turning cartwheels and French-braiding each other's hair when the ball was at the front line. Then when it came to them, they would cluster around and kick each other in the shins for a while before the ball popped out to be surrounded by a new cluster.

The game was always played against a background roar of what we called the "soccer daddies" and, to be fair, the occasional "soccer mommy." The adults always seemed more interested in the action than the girls did. Likewise, Lloyd Dubroff said that he had thought of the idea of the cross-country flight after being inspired by a similar odyssey by a little girl a few years ago. So whose dream was this? And who called *Good Morning America*? I'll bet Jessica didn't have their number.

Here's another question I've been hearing: What role did the media have in this tragedy? Our role was what it always is. We're supposed to let you know what is going on. Believe me, we don't ask people to plan outrageous stunts to get our attention. They think of that on their own.

And one more thing, my fellow big people. The media's role is to ask questions, better questions than anybody asked when we first heard about a seven-year-old child who was flying an airplane.

— April, 1996

THE SHORT, VALUABLE LIFE
OF ONE CHILD

THE NEWS WAS not good, but then we probably all knew it wouldn't be. He was so grievously hurt. Burns of the most serious kind covered his body.

Matthew Brent Richmond, twelve, died at nine twenty-two a.m. on a Monday morning.

Somebody packed up the balloons and posters and cards and notes sent to his hospital room. A Cub Scout troop wrote letters. So did some other kids and lots of adults. Strangers mostly. A radio station played his favorite song, "Midnight Cinderella," by Garth Brooks. People called the hospital every day to ask how he was doing.

You have to wonder if this was the most attention he ever got in his life. I wonder if he knew how much we were prepared to love him if we got another chance.

A woman who visited the boy at the hosptial told me that he was "pretty out of it." A nurse there says they keep badly burned patients "as comfortable as possible." I would guess that this means as many drugs as they can handle.

His mother's live-in boyfriend says he was bathing Matthew and burned him by accident. The mother defended the man at a bond hearing. These two waited more than thirteen hours to get help for Matthew after he was burned.

I have talked to as many people as I could find who knew this boy, shamelessly pumping them for infomation. It was, I promise you, out of respect for this child's life. I wanted him to be more than a "developmentally disabled twelve-year-old boy."

Everybody wanted to tell me things that sound like what we all say about every other victim. He was nice. He smiled a lot. That's almost worse than the developmental tag. I wanted better stuff, some boyish footprints left in this world.

Matt loved Grippo barbecue chips and Mountain Dew and listening to the Reds on the radio. He liked making cookies. "He made a mess with the egg, but it was worth it," a family friend says. "And don't you give people the idea that he was mute, that he couldn't talk."

What did he say? "Mama."

He liked Matchbox cars and made the requisite "vroom vroom" noises when he crashed them together.

"He was hyper and happy," another woman said. "I wish I had his energy." When you say that about a child, you usually mean you wish they'd meditate a little more.

Another woman, who helped out when Matthew was a baby, said she used to talk to him, forcing him to be still. "I wrapped my legs around him to keep him focused." Someone else said, "What a fighter. I can't believe he held on for so long." He struggled to live for twelve days.

Life must have been very precious to Matthew. Either that or he was just used to struggling. Everything he ever did was harder for him than for most kids. Walking. Talking. He was not a cardboard figure of a child. He was real, probably a handful at times.

What a dark story this is, except for the rather fine feelings Matthew Richmond roused in us. I wonder if they're real. And lasting. Will we remember his face when sides are to be taken? Will he remind us that we must take the child's side? Every time.

And that every single one of them should be treated as though there is no second chance.

— *January, 1997*

THE FRIENDLY STRANGER

THIS IS THE thinnest imaginable excuse to warn you again about your kids and strangers. For one thing, nothing terrible happened. A little girl cried a few tears, but she was not hurt. Only scared.

And I was the stranger. We know I am not dangerous, even if you get between me and the buffet line.

One recent weekend, my husband and I saw the movie *Tin Cup* at the Super Saver Cinema. Our theory is that a movie that is terrible for seven dollars is only pretty bad for a dollar and seventy-five cents. Popcorn there is superior to the National Amusements popcorn. Plus they give you refills.

Okay. Okay. I'm getting to the story, but I thought you might appreciate some atmosphere.

As we were walking down that long, dark hallway that

invites even the most law-abiding citizen to sneak into another movie, I heard a sniffle. A little girl, probably around five, was standing in the doorway of an empty theater.

"I can't find my mommy." Boy, have all of us heard that a time or two. Most of us remember saying it a time or two. But the world is a more sinister place than it once was. Especially for kids. A new federal study finds that child abuse is up. Shockingly up, nearly double the reported incidents from six years ago.

Most of it is not at the hands of strangers but at the hands of moms and dads and boyfriends and girlfriends and neighbors. And sometimes by strangers. Stranger can be a confusing notion to a little kid who doesn't know where to turn.

By the time I had dried this child's eyes and told her my name, we were no longer strangers. She would have gone anywhere with me. I could easily have told her we were going to look for her mommy in my car and she would have climbed inside.

And that's what scared me.

—WVXU radio,
October, 1996

DRESSING FOR THE PART

WHAT ARE WE to think of the death of this beauty queen? Or, more precisely, a beauty princess. This contestant, seen in pageants wearing a feather boa and dangling rhinestone earrings, was only six years old.

As the baffling events surrounding the murder of JonBenet Ramsey unfolded, America uneasily watched video images of this exquisite little girl posing in slinky evening gowns, her hair tinted a silvery blonde and elaborately coiffured.

The former Little Miss Colorado, from Boulder, was reportedly sexually assaulted. Her mouth was sealed with duct tape. Her skull was fractured. A white cord was around her neck. All this ugliness has been discussed against a background of, well, how she looked.

She looked like a little girl dressed as a woman, a very glamorous woman.

Her mother, Patricia, is a former beauty queen herself. She was Miss West Virginia in nineteen seventy-seven. Was she reliving her life through her daughter? How many hours a day did JonBenet spend having her hair moussed and styled? Why was this child wearing red lipstick and eyeliner and sequins and garden party hats?

This appears to be a perfect opportunity for sanctimony and judgment.

But the fact is, little JonBenet is not unusual. I'm not talking about all the other little girls who competed with her for the titles of Little Miss Charlevoix, Colorado State All-Star Kids Cover Girl, America's Royale Miss and National Tiny Miss Beauty.

Presumably they were outfitted and trained just like JonBenet, but just weren't as good at it.

Plenty of other children are forced to be adults every day, competing in more acceptable arenas. You can see it at swimming pools and in classrooms, on tennis courts and at computer keyboards and chessboards. And gymnasiums.

Ask Olympic gymnast Dominique Moceanu how old she was when somebody dressed her in a leotard and hoisted her up onto the balance beam. Ask figure skater Tai Babilonia how old she was when she started skating three or four times a day.

And we do not reserve the honor of early adulthood for little girls.

Picture the adorable Macauley Culkin of *Home Alone* (the first one) and as he is today, fending off his parents' attempts to suck up the profits from his work.

Or David Helfgott, real-life hero of the movie *Shine*. The young pianist collapses under the weight of his father's expectations and spends a decade in a mental hospital.

The little blonde girl in lipstick and sequins and high-heeled sling sandals really is not so different from some of the kids we see every day in jeans and pigtails, tiny athletes and computer nerds. JonBenet Ramsey was a child asked to perform as an adult.

She was simply dressed for the part.

— *January, 1997*

THE NOSY VILLAGE

LUCKILY, VICTOR CAVE is really cute. Gorgeous brown eyes with thick lashes. A nice smile. And outgoing, especially for a kid who just turned three. People in the neighborhood remembered him. Not to be overly dramatic, but maybe it saved his life.

He chatted with a couple of people in the grocery store, talked to some others on the street. One woman remembered him enough to worry.

She confronted the boy's mother, "Where is your baby?" Vela Dennis wanted to know.

It turns out that he was inside a nineteen seventy-five Cadillac Coupe deVille in the parking lot of an auto-repair shop. One of those big old gas hogs, the car is missing its hood ornament. Its once pale blue body is now a dull gray. At least the car is roomy, and the seats are leather. Cracked white leather.

I poked around the interior, but there wasn't much to see. Some mysterious (to me) car parts on the floor in back. It looked pretty clean and didn't smell bad. Some reports have Victor wrapped in a urine-soaked blanket.

Just in case it would matter to him, that he was trying to be a "big boy," I'd like to say that I saw absolutley no sign of that, even though police think his mother left him there for at least twelve hours.

The car's battery was missing, so Victor couldn't have honked the horn or turned on the lights to attract attention. Maybe he was asleep most of the time. So maybe he wasn't scared. Maybe.

A mechanic who left the lot at eleven thirty Saturday night swears that he would have seen Victor if he'd been in the car then. When police found the boy about ten a.m. Sunday, he was hungry and thirsty. Somebody bought him a sausage biscuit and egg sandwich and some juice. Victor said his mommy had left him there and would be back.

As usual and appropriate, the social workers draw a curtain between this little boy sent to their care and those of us who want to know more about him. They're friendly, polite. They just think it's more important to make life easier for Victor Cave than for me.

I admire that.

If the mother needs help, she may get it now. She's "in the system." Victor is with his father for the first time in two and a half years. And some people came forward to help a child who did not belong to them. A woman asked questions. A man made a telephone call to police. Somebody dug into his pocket for breakfast.

"People don't like to hear this, but it's that village thing again," one of the social workers says, "taking responsibility for kids who are too little to take care of themselves.

And it was not unbearably hot in the car. Or unbearably cold. If Victor's mom had put him there one month earlier or two months later, it might be a different story. But the weather wasn't bad, and the good villagers were on duty that morning.

Luckily.

— April, 1997